Mindset of the Warrior

Sport Psychology

Anthony Gilmour

Whole Mind Strategies
30 Cheam Street,
Dandenong North, Victoria, AUSTRALIA 3175

First Published 2021: Edition 1

This book is copyright. Apart from any fair dealing for the purpose of private study, research, criticism or review as permitted under the Copyright Act. No part of this book may be reproduced, stored in a retrieval system, communicated or transmitted in any form or by any means without prior written permission. All inquiries should be made direct to the author at email: info@wholemindstrategies.com.au

Cover design by Anthony Gilmour Illustrated by Tiana Lioulios
Published by Whole Mind Strategies

© Whole Mind Strategies Pty Ltd. All rights reserved.

ISBN-978-0-9875971-1-3 (paperback)
ISBN-978-0-9875971-0-6 (ebook – epub)

Dedication.

To all the volunteers around the world who give their time and effort to help children achieve their full potential in sport.

The true strength of human spirit: love, compassion and kindness. It is with us when we need to endure what seems unendurable. And it is found in the heart of man, not the head.

CONTENTS

Chapter 1: Introduction.   13

Chapter 2: The samurai and the Bushido Code   15

Chapter 3: Conscious v Subconscious Processing Power   21

Chapter 4: Consciousness   25

Chapter 5: Thinking, talking and memory as a function of consciousness   29

Chapter 6: Consciousness and what it is   37

Chapter 7: The monkey mind   43

Chapter 8: Hypnosis   49

Chapter 9: Understanding habits, needs and negative emotions   53

Chapter 10: The formation of many beliefs   53

Chapter 11: How the mind works   71

Chapter 12: The mind is a time machine   83

Chapter 13: Our judgements become our filters   87

Chapter 14: The essence of what we are   91

Chapter 15: We all live in an illusion   97

Chapter 16: The root of all craving   103

Chapter 17 How to release negative emotions   109

Chapter 18: Our suffering creates the motivation to change   115

Chapter 19: Purpose, Sociopaths, Integrity and Ethics   121

Chapter 20: Understanding the bully — 135

Chapter 21: Forgiveness — 141

Chapter 22: Ego states anchors and triggers — 145

Chapter 23: Comfort zones — 153

Chapter 24: Goal setting and time management — 159

Chapter 25: Unharnessed aggression — 167

Chapter 26: Attitude — 171

Chapter 27: Work ethic and training — 175

Chapter 28: Work and life balance — 179

Chapter 29: Culture and morale — 183

Chapter 30: Strategy, tactics and the 'Art of War' — 189

Chapter 31: Body language and presence — 205

Chapter 32: Self-talk and affirmations — 227

Chapter 33: Developing mindset — 231

Chapter 34 The bushido code for the modern warrior — 235

About the author — 241

ACKNOWLEDGMENTS

There are a number of people that we would like to acknowledge.

Chris Roering for his support and feedback.

Tiana Lioulios for her cover illustration.

My wife Julie for her proof reading and unconditional love.

George Sotiropolous for his feedback and our work together.

My children and Grandchildren who are all passionate about their sport.

All the sport psychology clients over the many years, your input has been invaluable.

All the good coaches I have come across both playing sport and coaching my children and grandchildren playing sport.

All the selfless people who devote their time and efforts volunteering at local sports clubs to make things happen. Without these people we would not have the depth of structure to build these exceptional athletes.

CHAPTER 1

Introduction

People of all sports, coaches, trainers and athletes will all benefit from reading this book. Much of it can be applied to personal life and business.

Anthony Gilmour is a psychotherapist who works as a mindset coach for athletes of all sports, business people and individuals suffering anxiety and depression. Tony worked in engineering most of his life with the last 5 years as managing director of a successful engineering company, before moving into the field of psychotherapy. For over 17 years Tony has been refining and testing programs to develop a positive mindset in people from all walks of life. Tony is the Author of the book 'Tragic to Magic', a book that gives an insight into how the mind works and how to live a happier life.

This book starts out defining the samurai mindset and the bushido code on which this mindset is founded. The author, by using simple principals and understandings begin to strip away the mystic and complexity of the psychology of the warrior. This gives a simple understanding of the mind of the samurai, before applying it to the modern day warrior, the athlete, in simple and effective ways.

Much of what you will read on the psychology aspect comes from Tony's previous book 'From Tragic to Magic'. This has been adapted for the athlete to gain an understanding of the warrior mindset.

The mind is neoplastic. If we focus on the negative we build more white matter (axons) between the right frontal cortex and the amygdala. (the flight or fight response area of the brain). When we focus on the positive it is the left side connections that grow. Greater white matter on the left side makes us more resilient to the negative things that happen in life. We bounce back quicker. This book is designed to build resilience in the athlete, emotionally not physically.

CHAPTER 2

The Samurai and the Bushido code

The Japanese samurai would have to be considered some of the greatest warriors of all time, and the meaning of the word 'samurai' is; "Those who serve in close attendance to the nobility." The samurai were the warrior class and they followed a set of rules known as Bushido. This set of rules, 'the Bushido code,' is a designed to influence the mindset and behaviour of a warrior. The samurai were not only the warriors of their feudal Lords; they were also the peace keepers and the policemen of an ancient society. The bushido code was designed as a moral code to create a mindset that gives integrity and purpose to their roles. Bushido is the way of the warrior, a unique philosophy that spread through the warrior class in Japan sometime after the 9th century.

When first looking at the bushido code, I was struck by its focus on moral behaviour to create a mindset. It is nothing to do with a fight mindset and more to do with moral principles to live by in daily life. The concept of bushido is chivalry.

With its beginnings in Neo-Confucianism it was also influenced by Shinto and Zen Buddhism, this allowed the violent life of the samurai to be balanced with wisdom and serenity. Although the bushido code seems to stress loyalty, frugality, martial arts mastery and honor until death, its basic moral principles go much further than this. It is much more than having the ultimate aim in life being; to die a good death with one's honour intact. The way of the warrior is moral guide to living life. Depending on who you read, it is said are seven or eight virtues of Bushido. There are also some associated virtues. For simplicity, we will endeavor to combine them into eight basic virtues that make up the bushido code of chivalry. The eight virtues are: Rectitude or justice, Courage, Benevolence and mercy, Politeness and respect, Honesty and sincerity, Honour, Loyalty and Character and self-control: The foundation of the warrior mindset. We will look into the foundation because without good foundations the building is weak.

Rectitude or justice

Rectitude can be described as morally correct thinking and behaviour - Integrity; honesty; righteousness; straightforwardness. This is considered the strongest virtue of the bushido code, the virtue on which all others rest. This is the corner stone of bushido. Rectitude is the power to decide on a course of action in accordance with reason and logic. As one well know samurai puts it: To die when to die is right, to strike when to strike is right. Another says that without rectitude, neither talent nor learning can make a man into a samurai. The corner stone in rational and logical behavior must have its basics in how we think, moral conviction and ethics.

Benevolence and Mercy

Benevolence and mercy are acts of kindness and the desire to do good for others; goodwill towards others and charitableness. It is often said that the highest requirement of a ruler of men is benevolence. Be it ruler or a samurai, with the position comes power over others; the power to command and the power over life and death. This must be equally balanced with the powers of benevolence and mercy. Love, affection for others, generosity, compassion and sympathy are traits of benevolence. To be forgiving of insults and injury and free from petty resentfulness or vindictiveness, to be magnanimous and noble of mind is the mindset of the samurai.

Courage

Courage is doing what is right, and this is the difference between bravery and courage in the bushido code. Courage is a virtue if it is employed through the virtue of rectitude. Knowing what is right and not doing it displays a lack of courage. The samurai lived daily with the courage of his convictions. A person can be brave and yet still lack courage to do the right thing. It was this courage through the virtue of rectitude that made the samurai fearless.

Politeness and Respect

Respect is esteem and a sense of worth for another person or a person's position. This virtue is based in benevolence with regards to the feelings of others. Being polite and respectful is not to be done just for the sake of good manners but as a benevolent regard for the feelings of others. The samurai were known to be polite and respectful even to their enemies. A defeated foe was usually treated with the greatest respect.

Honesty and Sincerity

Honesty and sincerity is the freedom from deceit, hypocrisy, or duplicity in intention, action and communication. It is being truthful upright and fair. It is said that the samurai had little interest in money, luxury or material things. They encouraged thrift and simplicity and abstinence. The samurai mindset was to serve others not to serve themselves. Luxury was seen as a threat to manhood and severe simplicity was required of the samurai. It was thought that money and luxury would only corrupt the samurai mindset.

Honour

Honour is honesty, or integrity in one's beliefs and actions. Honour not only as a warrior, but also in non-martial behavior. A sense of honour is a sense of personal dignity and worth. The samurai was born and bred to value the privileges and duties of his profession. Fear of disgrace was a motivating force behind honorable actions. It is the reason many samurai committed suicide after defeat in battle. The disgrace from failing in their duties could only be appeased by honorable death. The aim of the samurai was to die a good death in the service of their master with their honour intact.

Loyalty

True men and women remain loyal to the people they are indebted to. It is faithfulness to commitments and obligations. In the mind of the samurai, it is through the importance of honour that lies at the core of loyalty. Loyalty to a superior was a virtue of the samurai. A gang of criminals can be loyal to one another, but only in honour does loyalty assume such importance and self-control.

Character and self-control

The moral and ethical qualities of a person make up their character. Qualities of honesty, courage and integrity form a person's character. The first objective of a samurai's education was to build up character. Bushido teaches a moral standard of rules for the behaviour of the samurai to build character and self-control. Compassion over confrontation and benevolence over belligerence were seen as manly, not weak. It was expected the samurai should know the difference between what is right and what is wrong in both thinking and action. Even being impatient and quick to anger was seen as poor self-control and of inferior character. Unharnessed aggression was seen as a weakness. It is this building of character through the moral compass of bushido that creates the warrior mindset of the samurai. It is a mindset without doubt or fear; without indecision; through virtues of rectitude or justice – courage - benevolence and mercy - politeness and respect - honesty and sincerity – honour - loyalty - character and self-control.

Some of these were not the virtues I expected to find in my search for the warrior mindset, but as you go through this book I will tie them all together through an understanding of modern psychological principals.

Unharnessed aggression is one of the biggest detriments to creating a winning mindset in any sport. Seen as a weakness for the samurai, it is also a weakness for the athlete. The bushido code was designed to create a balanced mind, free from unharnessed aggression and fear. I stopped looking at the samurai mindset from the point of a soldier in a feudal and divided country; and moved to the point of a virtuous servant of his master and people. I believe that this is where the mindset was created.

I will use examples from a number of sports because this book about the warrior mindset is about the athlete, and can be used in any sport. First we must understand the mind from a modern day psychological point of view. What it is that makes us tick?

CHAPTER 3

Conscious v Subconscious processing power

The subconscious mind can process 20 000 000 bits of info per second. The conscious mind will generally process 100 to 150 bits of info/sec.

So the subconscious mind can process 500, 000 times more information per second than the conscious mind is able to. This according to information from the book: 'The Biology of Belief' by Dr. Bruce Lipton a cellular biologist.

Another study suggests that the subconscious impulses travel at a speed of up to 100,000 mph! Compare this to your conscious mind where impulses travel at only 100-150 mph. We have 50 trillion cells in our body performing trillions of processes – so an enormous processing power is required. In other words, it is as if roughly 10'000 cinema films are actually going on in the brain all at once, while we are only consciously aware of one of them. Altogether then, the data rate processed by the brain is an astronomical 320 Gb/s!

Researchers at the University of Pennsylvania School of medicine, estimate the human retina can transmit visual input at 10 million bits per second. See below other results for all five senses.

Eyes (vision): 10,000,000 bits per second

Ears (hearing): 100,000 bits per second

Skin (touch): 1,000,000 bits per second

Nose (smell): 100,000 bits per second

Mouth (taste): 1,000 bits per second

Thus, in total we receive through our five senses more than 11 million bits of information each second of the day, while our conscious mind can only deal with one subject at a time at a rate of less than 150 bits per second. That's another very good reason why we need our subconscious to process the information from our senses, we would go mad (and we mean that literally) if all that information came straight to our conscious mind.

Our conscious mind can only deal with less than 0.002 % of all information coming in; only about 0.002% of all the brain's activity is experienced consciously.

What does this all mean for the athlete?

The subconscious doesn't think, it reacts, based on preconditioned programming. Or if we see it as a computer; the programming we have developed and fine-tuned through repetition, these become habits and habits are automatic programs. We have both physical programs and emotional programs.

The conscious mind sets the goal with an expectation and the subconscious performs the task. Brain and body are not separate but interconnected. Modern science tells us the subconscious is both brain and body.

CONSCIOUSNESS V SUBCONSCIOUS PROCESSING POWER

Perception comes through the senses, but can be coloured to give a distorted reality through emotion, based on past judgements of experiences. This perception through repetition of thought can become beliefs. Seeing *is not* believing; what we believe is what we see.

The ego, as I define it, is the base of our emotionally created programs based on fear, designed to protect us from further pain. The fears are the wants for control, approval, security and escape. These fears are impossible to satisfy because they are irrational and illogical. The subconscious is neither rational nor logical. The wants are an attachment to an outcome.

The conscious mind processes information at around 100 to 150 bits per second, processing possible futures and sometimes scanning the past to fine tune decision making in the present. The subconscious processes 20,000,000 bits of information per second in real time based on past programming.

Example: A cricketer, close in the field of play scans the future possibility of the ball coming his way. He then has a quick scan back to past positive experience (developing strategy). He then comes back to the moment and surrenders to the subconscious with a positive expectation because he has no idea where the ball will go. The ball heads down to the batsman. The subconscious is now processing ball speed, batsman's movement's stance and swing all in real time. The ball is hit, a hand goes out and the fingers curl around the ball as it hits the palm of the hand, all in a split second. The conscious mind only kicks in with the acknowledgment of the catch after it is over.

Imagine now the same situation. The conscious mind scanning back to the last dropped catch and the future possibility of another dropped catch planting the seeds of doubt and want. This will interrupt the subconscious expectation and interfere with its reaction and flow of information to muscle memory.

Imagine now the same situation. The conscious mind scanning back to the last dropped catch. A realisation he needs to adjust his position. Accepting this lesson and then leaving it in the past where it belongs. Refocus in the present with a positive expectation the problem is resolved.

The conscious mind gets in the road when we think too much; and this is true for an athlete in any sport. It interrupts the natural conditioned flow of information from the subconscious to muscle memory. *Repetition is the mother of skill; skill is a programmed response; a habit.*

Negative emotions - Fears.

Negative emotions are fears that can be broken down into the want for approval, control, security and escape. We were not born with these fears. They are conditioned fears. They are also irrational and illogical because they are impossible to achieve on a continuing basis. They are impossible to satisfy. They create most of our emotional unrest and problems. They have no purpose. We will discuss the wants in a later chapter.

Confidence.

Confidence follows trust and trust follows confidence. Trust in your skill set, including your developing psychological mind set will give unshakable confidence. Understand that your opponents have an ego to contend with. Their own fears and wants. They have their own doubts. This can be exploited. Confidence comes from the lack of wants and the creation of a positive expectation.

CHAPTER 4

Consciousness

> *What is it that differentiates us from all other living creatures on this wonderful planet we call mother earth?*

Surely all creatures are conscious at some time or other. What is different between my conscious waking hours, from the moment I flicker into conscious life as I awake from my slumber to the time the light goes out each night as I drift into sleep. This can't be called consciousness without marrying this attribute to all living things. Is the bird not conscious as it heralds in the morning light. Being conscious and human consciousness is not the same thing. Is the plant not conscious as it unfolds its petals to the morning sun. An interesting thought. How does the plant know when to blossom without being conscious of its environment? I suppose the best place to start is to look at what consciousness isn't.

I am barely conscious of the birds calling to each other in the background as I type these words unless I stop and take notice. But as soon as I take notice the garden springs to life with birds full of song. I am certainly conscious of the next door neighbour as he fires his lawn mower into life, disturbing my peace and tranquillity.

If we look at some definitions of consciousness it becomes more confusing. One definition states it is a quality or state of awareness, or, of being aware of an external object or something within oneself. Using this definition we can picture the plants awareness of the morning sun on its leaves and assume it has consciousness. Or the gazelle startled by the rustling grass as the lion makes its move. I think we can safely state there is a reactive consciousness to one's environment that all living things possibly possess, but this is quite a bit different to what we might call our uniquely human consciousness. So let's take look at this in more detail.

Just how much consciousness do we have during each and every day? I think you might be surprised to find that we spend much of our day in reactive consciousness, and very little of the day in what we will call human consciousness.

I awake in the morning and slip from my bed, although sometimes it seems I drag myself from my bed or at other times I jump from my bed; which is often determined by the amount and quality of sleep, and the things I expect to experience in the day ahead. I then go straight to the shower where I wash then dry myself before brushing my hair and teeth. Next it is on to the wardrobe where I chose the clothes to wear based usually on the weather and functions of the day ahead. I then get dressed and head downstairs for a coffee. The laptop is turned on and I download my emails for the day while drinking my morning coffee. How much of this process am I aware of consciously? Very little. I have done things the same way for years. I suppose I consciously choose to get out of bed and I consciously choose what clothes to wear but most of the rest of my actions are done from subconscious habit. I wash and dry in much the same way, brush my hair and teeth in much the same way and dress myself the same way day after day. Socks before pants, right foot before left foot and all without a conscious thought. In my mind I may be thinking about the day ahead or reviewing the day before but there is little awareness of the things I am doing. I am doing things from the automatic pilot of the subconscious mind. Even driving to work, unless there is some specific incident out of the ordinary that grabs my attention requiring a change in behaviour, the subconscious is driving the car. I am not actually conscious of my hands on the steering wheel as it moves to the left and right, or the foot on the accelerator governing my speed or the foot that seems to automatically depress the brake pedal with just the right pressure when needed. To highlight this point I can give a simple example. I recently bought my wife a Peugeot car. I drive a Toyota. The indicator levers are on different sides of the steering wheel in these two cars. On the odd occasion when I drive my wife's car the windscreen wipers spring to life when I indicate due to my old habit. I have to consciously make a choice to use the opposite lever to avoid this. Old habits die hard.

When it comes to the performance of motor skills, we can see that consciousness is not only unnecessary, but is probably a hindrance to the process which is a result of automatic inferences by our nervous system. A problem I see all the time in sport performance issues. It is said that the subconscious is processing 20,000,000 bits of information per second, and the conscious mind is processing 100 to 150 bit of information per second. Whatever the actual figure might be, we do know the subconscious is performing at a much faster speed than the speed with which we think. This leads us to the question – Is thinking consciousness?

CHAPTER 5

Thinking, talking and memory as a function of consciousness.

I suppose that it is easy to assume that all thinking is a part of consciousness but is it?

What is thinking and how much of thinking are we really conscious of?

If we look at the number of definitions of thinking we can find, we again come across many varieties of flowers in a garden of uncertainty. Here are some definitions that can be found through a simple internet search.

A way of reasoning; judgment.

To have a conscious mind, to some extent of reasoning, remembering experiences, making rational decisions, etc.

The action of using one's mind to produce thoughts.

The process of considering or reasoning about something.

Reasoning seems to play a key part in the definition of consciousness but are we really conscious of reasoning? Let's start at the start of thinking. We must start with a thought about something to reason about before we can begin reasoning. With this in mind we must start with an initial instruction to the mind on what to think about, and the parameters and materials on which the thinking and therefore the reasoning is to operate.

This initial instruction might be a reaction to external stimuli or changing conditions.

If we use the example of my arranging a game of golf at the weekend. My friend Stuart called and asked if I would like to play at 2:00pm on Saturday. The first instruction to my mind was ' Do I have anything else on'. The reasoning came back that there was nothing of importance on that afternoon and I agreed to play. Thinking again about it that morning I gave another instruction to the mind, "What time to leave home'. I reasoned that it would take 20 minutes to drive there and 10 minutes to pull on my golf shoes, set up the golf bag and allow for any issues with traffic. ' Leave at 1:30pm' was the answer that came back. Just how much of this thinking was conscious and how much of the thinking and reasoning was subconscious. I suppose we can argue that the initial instruction was conscious but it can also be argued that it was a reaction to changing stimuli. But what actually happened in the thinking process after the initial instruction?

After the initial instruction, which is a bit like a google search, the thinking was handed to the subconscious and it scanned the mind for all possibilities and probabilities. It then reasoned that there was no reason not to go to golf and at what time to go; this was given automatically. I was not conscious of the process or the reasoning, just the answer.

So, thinking it would seem is an automatic process following an instruction to the mind, this instruction will construct a conclusion based on reasoning that is also subconsciously generated.

But what if we accept the reasoning without question? What if our reasoning is faulty and based on instructions that limit the parameters and materials to end up with a judgment that isn't true, but we accept it as true. There seems to be a part that we often miss in thinking; the testing of reasoning through logic. Logic is the science of justification of conclusions we have reached through natural reasoning. The reason we need logic at all is because most reasoning is not conscious at all. Our minds work faster than conscious reasoning can keep up.

Critical thinking is the use of logic to critique the reasoning that the subconscious is presenting us with. But just how much critical thinking do we employ in our day to day life. I think we tend to employ it more in our working thinking than our personal thinking.

All the brilliant minds in history from Albert Einstein to Thomas Edison have had something in common. They have all said that they start with thinking about the problem and at some time later, the answer seems to materialise magically into the mind. It is said that Einstein's theory of relativity came to him while looking out the window, day dreaming on a train. Edison used to take daily naps and wake with the answer blossoming in mind. Of course, logic would have to check the conclusion before accepting it.

Most of the issues we come across in sport psychotherapy will be issues created in the clients mind by their limited instructions to the thinking process, and the lack of logic to check the subconscious reasoned conclusions. The lack of logic will create erroneous judgments that can form into erroneous beliefs. What they believe is what they will see. Much of a person's negative thinking must be habitual and subconscious.

Let's take the example of a client that came to me because of his depression. We will use the name John for confidentiality reasons. John was a 30 year old building construction supervisor who was finding it hard to drag himself from the bed or couch. He had a good relationship with his wife and two young children he adored, but his first statement to me was 'my life is shit'. He had become apathetic and unmotivated. John had bought a house on a large block of land and subdivided the land. He was in the process of building second house on the subdivided land and he said that this was about 90% finished. There was no mortgage on either property and he had more than enough funds in the bank to complete the second house with plenty in reserve. I often look for regret, disappointment or guilt as a reason for depression, or a lack of good relationships but this didn't seem to be the case here. Or was it?

I pointed out that our thinking is usually the cause of depression or anxiety and went on to teach him choice theory to show him he can think differently. His reply was 'I already know everything you have just told me but is doesn't change the fact that my life is shit'. The following is roughly what the conversation comprised of after this statement.

I said to John ' You look healthy enough, your life might be shit if you were dying of some painful disease'.

' Yea, I'm healthy'. Said John

' You say you have a good relationship' I said. 'Life might be shit if you had a bad relationship'.

'I have a good relationship and my wife is very supportive' John said.

' Two beautiful kids and both healthy, your life might be shit if one of your children had an incurable disease'. I continued on.

' Both kids are healthy, that's not the problem. Work is shit' John replied.

THINKING, TALKING, AND MEMORY AS A FUNCTION OF CONSCIOUSNESS

' Life might be shit if you didn't have a job and were having trouble finding one' was my reply.

'People don't do the right thing and it pisses me off' was Johns reply.

'If people did the right thing there would be no need for a supervisor and you wouldn't be getting paid more than they do to keep them on track' was my reply.

John looked at me for a moment and said ' So every time I say something is shit you will find something good about it'?

I told John his life wasn't shit, he was just looking at it through shit coloured glasses.

> **The instructions to the mind is like a Google search. It looks for everything that agrees with the search instructions.**

Johns instruction to his mind was that his life was shit. Handing this to the subconscious, his mind hunted for all the negative things in his life and deleted out all the positives. He was googling his instruction to his mind that his life was shit. This was the parameters and materials he instructed his mind to reason on. The subconscious reasoning was faulty. John took this faulty reasoning as true because he didn't employ logic to test it. I just applied logic to point out the faulty reasoning.

This is also true in sport. If you instruct your mind that you are not good enough; the mind will find all the reasons in the past to accept this instruction and reason that it is true. It will not look at all the times you have been successful and triumphed because the instruction to the mind and its parameters filter out anything that doesn't agree with this judgement. If you tell yourself you are good enough; your mind will look for all the times you have excelled and been successful. Whatever seeds you plant in your mind will grow to give fruit. It is the universal law of cause and effect. What you sow so shall you reap. If you sow bitter seeds it will be a bitter harvest.

Your instruction in to your mind will create a construction based on the parameters you have given it. Unless you apply logic to analyze the reasoning, you are performing on faulty reasoning. It is all self-hypnosis, positive of negative, continued self-suggestions. *See this like a google search of the mind. If you say you can, the mind looks for all the reasons why you can. If you say you can't, the mind looks for all the reasons why you cant.*

Speaking as a function of consciousness.

Are we conscious of what we say? Speaking is just a habit of connecting letters, which form words, which then form a sentence. First we learn words by observing what others are using to describe something. This becomes our basis for perception and communication. We start to use their words. As our language skills grow our perception of our world grows. Our language is the basis of our perception of the world.

The skills we are learning to put words and sentences together are habitual and therefore subconscious in its operation. The biggest problem with public speaking, one of the greatest phobias in the world, is, if we think too much about what we are going to say we get stuck trying to say it. With our friends and family we don't think about what we are going to say, we just say it. No problem.

I used to spend time before a seminar planning and rehearsing what I would say, lots of notes to keep me on track, and I managed to get through but it was an uncomfortable experience. One time I arranged a seminar and the speaker didn't turn up. I had to cover by giving a seminar myself, and without notes or rehearsal gave the most comfortable seminar I had ever given. I didn't think about what I had to say I just said it. It was all coming from the subconscious, and from my basic instruction to my mind about what to talk about. I wasn't trying to remember what to say, I was just saying what I thought I should say.

THINKING, TALKING, AND MEMORY AS A FUNCTION OF CONSCIOUSNESS

Memory as a function of consciousness

Do we exhibit consciousness because we remember? Our memories seem like a collage of movies and pictures that represent our past experience; but are they a true representation of what happened?

If I ask you to see yourself in a happy memory, maybe at a beach, river or lake as you are about to jump into the water. What do you see?

Most people will see themselves at the beach and see what they are wearing and the people around them. They might even feel the trepidation of jumping into the cold water. How can this be true? When you were there you didn't see yourself, you just experienced it from within, so how can this memory be true? They are not true memories, they are constructed; based on the parameters given to the mind. The mind finds an engram of the memory, a snapshot so to speak, it then constructs a memory and places you in it. This is the reason why the police can interview 6 witnesses to an incident and all the memories will be slightly different. If two recollections are exactly the same the police will suspect collusion. Interesting!

Now we know we can't really trust most of our memories. Most memories are constructed subconsciously and we are not conscious of the differences between the construction and reality. The mind has reasoned that this is the memory and you accept it without question. You might be wondering at this stage what is true and what is not? What is real and what is fantasy.

> **I think we can safely conclude that we are not fully conscious of all** *thinking, speaking or memory.*

CHAPTER 6

Consciousness and what it is.

If I ask you to imagine the country you live in. You will probably see the shape of the country and the cities and where they are located. What you are really seeing is a map of the country. You have seen this before but you have not seen the whole country before with your own eyes.

> *The map is an analogy of the country. It has a similar shape but it is not the country, it is not the territory.*

What have we done mentally here?

We have created a space in our minds eye, a place in space that resides nowhere in particular. We then project an analogy of our country in this space which is an analogy of the true country. From our instruction to our mind we create an imagined construction based on the parameters given. Let's look back now at the memory section where we place ourselves in the memory. This is just an analogy of ourselves in the real world, we also create this analogy of ourselves in an imaginary world that is just an analogy of the real world. We then metaphorically move around this imaginary world using an analogy of ourselves. So the map is not the territory, it represents the territory.

How can we build this fantasy world in our minds eye, when no other living thing on the planet can? Our advanced language. The use of analogies and metaphors to generate an imaginary world based on our real life experiences. We create an analogy of the world and of ourselves and move about metaphorically within it.

We have become self-conscious by building a fantasy world based on what we think is happening in the real world; but most of it is a fantasy.

So we are living in the real world and a fantasy world at the same time. We see the real world through the filter of our fantasy world. Now this is where it becomes interesting. The story of John in the last chapter should shows us how our fantasy world can start to become our reality, unless we apply some logic to our reasoning and test it.

The Narrative

The instructions to the mind is our narrative, our self-talk. This is self-hypnosis, self-suggestion. This is the true creator or our future. The instruction is the narrative and the construction is the fantasy based on the narrative. To use an analogy, The projected analogy of 'I' is the main actor, the narrative is a the director, and the fantasy is the movie. The movie will then become our reality. If your narrative is drama you are creating a drama movie, if it is adventure, you are creating and adventure movie. So many people are creating a horror story without even knowing it.

I see my world as an adventure and a comedy. I am continually looking for the next adventure such as this book, or laughing at things that go wrong. I am not naturally a romantic person but will often shift my perception to this and create more romance. After over 30 years of marriage you need to keep creating the relationship and the world you would like to live in.

As an example of the narrative we can use. For years my wife and I have been telling each other and ourselves that we have the best relationship of anyone we know. When you consider that I like my own space and my wife is a very social person, that I have interests she has no interest in and vice versa. It is hard to understand why we have such a good relationship. It is the narrative we use; and people tell us all the time what a good relationship we have. The fantasy becomes our reality.

Many of the thoughts we have are habitual and therefore coming from the subconscious. Conscious mind is only applied when we instruct our mind to think within conscious logical parameters and check the reasoning though logic. Continued instructions of the same type will eventually become habitual ways of thinking. There is nothing wrong with this if the habits of thinking are beneficial and positive in outcome.

In sport, no-one who has achieved great things has done so without creating the fantasy in their own minds about achieving great things. Every Olympic champion has seen themselves winning gold, bursting through the tape at the end of a run, slotting in the goal that wins the competition or the thundering volley that claims victory. Every world champion has seen themselves as a world champion long before they achieved it. The narrative and fantasy proceeded the achievement and the achievement was a result of the narrative and fantasy. They don't use a narrative that destroys hope and belief, they use a narrative that feeds and nurtures it. Affirmations are instructions to the mind that creates a fantasy of great things to come but affirmations alone won't win the competition. It is the daily narrative minute to minute that creates great things. It is the continual positive narrative that makes this type of thinking habitual. The winning mindset is a habitual positive mindset that creates a habitual way of seeing the world. A fantasy? Yes, but one that will become a reality over time. Habits can take time to get rid of and time to develop, but there is no habit stronger than the mind that created it. Think big, dream big and let your dreams become reality.

| Instruction | - | Construction | - | Reality |
| *Narrative* | - | *Fantasy* | - | *Reality* |

What we have just investigated is the creative mechanism of the mind. It is how we perceive our life, how we live our life and how we create our future. We are all seeing the real world through our own imaginary world for much of the time.

If we look at an example of this.

The narrative of a boxer or mixed martial arts fighter.

Pre-fight narrative and construction.

Fighter No 1.

Narrative

This opponent is bigger and has a longer reach than me. He has won his last two fights. This will be a hard fight to win.

Construction including reasoning.

The mind looks for all the reasons to be afraid and why the fight will be hard. Better be afraid of his reach, he could knock me out and I could get hurt. Better keep out of his way is the reasoning that comes back.

Not tested by logic.

He has won two out of the last four fights and you have won four. You have beaten taller fighters with longer reaches in the past without a problem. He should be more afraid of your record than you should be of his.

Reality.

CONSIOUSNESS AND WHAT IT IS

Fighter No 1 fights defensively, doesn't follow his strategy and loses on points and doesn't fight to the best of his ability. This fighter has trained his subconscious mind and body to fight but the fearful thoughts and doubts interfere with the messages from the subconscious to muscle memory. He continually second guesses himself. I often call this paralysis by over analysis: Thinking too much. The fearful thoughts create anxiety and the anxiety drains energy.

Fighter No 2.

Narrative.

He is bigger and with a longer reach but I have beaten people like this before. He has only won two of his last four fights and I have won the last four. I have the experience, skills and fitness to finish this guy off.

Construction.

The mind looks for all the reasons to agree with the instruction and comes up with; I have beaten taller guys with longer reaches and I can beat him. My winning record is better than his and he had better be afraid.

Logically correct

Reality.

He sticks confidently to his strategy and fights to the best of his ability. Gives himself the best possible outcome. He is not second guessing himself and allows his subconscious mind and body to perform at the optimum level of his training and fitness.

We are looking at the real world through an imaginary world that is created in our belief system. A filter system based on our beliefs, judgements and fears. This imaginary world is an analogy of the real world, it is created through our language to describe the world we see.

The imaginary world will eventually become our reality by the way we think and act.

If we look back now to the Bushido code. Simple instructions to the mind about a code of ethics, a foundation on which to build action. They were taught to think or more importantly, KNOW, before they were allowed to act. Their lack of fear can be attributed to this powerful trained narrative. This narrative eventually becomes a habit of thinking, a habit of knowing what to do. The mind was programmed to be fearless. They had programed themselves not to entertain fearful thoughts. The instructions creates the fantasy, the fantasy eventually becomes reality.

CHAPTER 7

The Monkey Mind

The human mind.

If we take a simplistic view of the brain of a human being. The thing that seems to set us apart from other animals on this amazing planet is the pre-frontal cortex. The part of the brain behind the forehead. It is larger in human beings than in other animals.

This part of the brain develops as we grow and around the age of seven we start to develop a rational logical part of the mind as our language grows more complex. We can also call this part of the mind the human mind because it is the difference between us and animals of lesser intelligence. This part of the mind is genetically encoded into us at birth and is the seat of consciousness as we know it. It is this consciousness that allows us to feel love and compassion with the exception of sociopaths, many of whom operate without a conscience and feel little love of compassion for others. Recent studies have concluded that this may be a genetic issue.

The computer

The bulk of the brain seems to be more like a blank computer hard drive at birth that starts to store programs as we learn. Many of these programs are learned habits that work from a subconscious level. As explained in previous chapters, much of our thinking, speaking etc. is subconscious. It is the storage place of all our learned skills and beliefs, our habits of thinking and acting.

The monkey mind or the chimp.

The older part of the brain; the limbic system is what we seem to have most in common with other animals. The reptilian, mammalian brain. This is the seat of our fear response. The flight or fight response. We can call this the monkey mind or the chimp. There are differences between males and females in this part of the brain. This part of the brain allows the chimp to survive in the jungle.

Chimps like to live in troops; it gives the chimp a better chance of survival. If you get kicked out of the troop you have much less of a chance of surviving the threats of the jungle. Human beings also like to be a part of a troop, be it family, friends, clubs and associations.

The male chimps are vying for power. This is the 'survival of the fittest' in action. The strongest chimp will have its pick of females and he has billions of sperm to spend in generating his offspring. Male chimps protect the chimp territory from other groups of chimps or from other predators.

The female chimps protect the nest and offspring. They can be very vigilant when the male chimps are not around. The female chimp has only one egg per month and is particular in who she will allow to fertilise it. The female chimp will go for the strongest male chimp but if she thinks there is a strong up and coming younger chimp, she may mate with both to give her offspring a better chance of survival.

We can see the chimp mind at work in many human situations. Criminal gangs are usually comprised of men fighting other groups of men for territory and power. This is the chimp mindset at work. In women, the home is the nest and they can be very protective of their offspring, genetically more maternal, usually. I often remove the six cushions off the bed at night that have no practical purpose other than decoration, and I often wonder if this is my wife nesting. A single mans room would usually be sparse, a single women's room would be full of memories.

Our body language is usually coming from the subconscious chimp and the aggressive posturing of some men is much like the silver backed gorilla banging his chest. It is also interesting to note that a woman has three times more flirting body language than a man. It is the woman who is choosing the partner, not the guys. Women are still subconsciously drawn to power. Whether it be a young girl marrying an older rich man for security, or women drawn to celebrity, be it in sport or entertainment. Power can be perceived in different forms. A strong personality, lots of confidence, good sense of humour or successful in business. The chimp is not a rational or logical mind.

Have you ever had some time in your life when you possibly lost your temper, and a short while later were regretting what you said or did?

'Why did I do that, why did I say that?'

It wasn't you that said it or did it, it was the chimp. When the chimp jumps out of the box it can overpower the human mind because it is five time stronger and faster than the human mind. So, our primal instincts of survival can often dominate our thinking, but most perceived threats are not real physical threats. There is very rarely a life or death situation creating these perceived threats. If we let the chimp run the show we can create problems.

The chimp plants programs in the computer from an early age. We can be scared of the dark as a child and my first memory is of a witch at the top of our stairs, just outside my bedroom. It was just a shadow, but it was a witch to me. No matter how many time my mother told me it was a shadow, the Witch was still there. I was no older than five years of age and the Witch disappeared when we moved house at the age of five.

Eventually, the logical rational mind begins to overwrite the old programs and the child understands the fear is not real, but in the first seven or so years we don't have this protection. We believe in Santa Clause, the Easter bunny and the Witch at the top of the stairs. Sadly, Many adults are still operating from perceived threats generated by the chimp. We need the chimp. The chimp mind is the part of your mind that get you to duck when a ball is heading towards your head, it is quicker than the human mind and will get you out of harm's way. Now the interesting thing here is that the computer, subconscious programming, is twenty times faster than the chimp. With the right programs the chimp will stay in its box.

Now we can't get rid of the chimp and we don't want to, it has its purpose in life threatening situations. We must learn to manage the chimp. Most anxieties are not life threatening but the chimp sees them as life threatening and brings in the flight or fight response.

In sport the chimp is very destructive. It watches the scoreboard, gets angry and petulant. The chimp is looking for threats and misses opportunities. The chimp unbalances the mind and creates problems. The chimp looks at what you can't do not what you can do. All great athletes have to contend with the chimp at some time or other. There is a thing in golf called 'the yips'. The yips is where a person is thinking so much about the playing of the shot that their shots become jumpy and not fluid. They are stuck in the swing and not focused on the target. Once it starts it can become a nightmare for the player. Most athletes with the yips start to think about what they think they need to do instead of doing it. In golf I call this stuck in the swing. Is the back swing right, or the follow through? Am I coming over my elbow in the backswing and keeping it close to my body? Are my feet in the right position? Interrupting the messages from the subconscious to the body and the result is painful. Then the anger starts. Now the chimp is out of the box and the frustrations build with every shot.

THE MONKEY MIND

> **We can't get rid of the chimp but we can manage it.**

In finishing this chapter I would just like to mention that some of the toughest and strongest people I have ever met are the most sensitive. There is a difference between being strong or hard.

A strong man or woman will feel comfortable being themselves. They feel love and compassion for others. They are strong because their integrity is strong. They feel confident being themselves.

A hard man or woman tend not to be sensitive, or if they seem so it is to suit other purposes. They lack conscience and feel no remorse or regret. They can be your best friend if it pays off in some way but will discard you when you are no benefit for them. Most will be aggressive or often angry when things don't go their way, this comes from the chimp mind.

The strong person will have the integrity that comes from the human mind and in most cases will keep the chimp in check. When they allow the chimp to take over they can create big problems for themselves and others if they don't arrest it. Guilt, self-loathing, disappointment and regret are common. Now they feel weak.

Hard men and women don't want to change. They see life as a battle and want to be the victor. Everything is about conquest and not living just for livings sake.

Strong people are pliable, they bend around the differences in people. Hard people are brittle, there is no give.

This begs the question. Where Samurai hard or strong?

The hard person acts for themselves. The Samurai has only actions for others. The hard persons integrity is determined by what they can get out or it. The strong persons integrity is unwavering and based on a code of ethics. A strong person will bend and a hard person will break.

The best people are like Samurai swords. The body is softer and multi-layered, it will endure a fight and bend but not break. The edge is hardened to cut and maintain sharpness even if it chips.

The body and mind is the discipline and training. The edge is the conscious focus of the human logical mind.

Training in the Bushido code of virtues was designed to harness the monkey mind by programing the computer through the human mind.

CHAPTER 8

Hypnosis

All hypnosis is self-hypnosis. People have this misconception that hypnosis is about controlling someone else's mind. What a load of rubbish. You can't make a person do anything against their better values. You can get a person to do something if the alternative is better than their current situation, but the subconscious is a protective mechanism. It won't accept anything that conflicts with your current beliefs unless it sees a benefit. If you could control another person, an unethical hypnotist could tell you to rob a bank and bring the money to them. They would retire in a month and leave you with the consequences. Hypnosis or a better way of looking at this is Clinical Hypnotherapy, is a tool to enter a person's analogy of the world and plant suggested analogies and metaphors beneficial to the client to overcome problems in their thinking.

Our self-talk is self-hypnosis. Our narrative is self-suggestion. I think the hardest part for a therapist is to overcome the continual negative self-hypnosis that people are using on themselves. Their own self-suggestion.

I mentioned earlier that our narrative creates our fantasy and the fantasy becomes our reality. Self-suggestion is our narrative. If the chimp highjacks the narrative or the suggestions are usually fearful. It's just a protective mechanism; not you.

My work is psychotherapy. Hypnotherapy is just a tool in the tool box. I strongly believe that without the understanding of how and what you create, that hypnotherapy will not change the habits of the mind long term, the old habits will try to reassert their dominance. I will also say that I have been surprised at how quick changes can be made through hypnotherapy. If there is an engram created at a time of trauma this can often be reframed and resolved, often in a single session, and the emotion tied to it dissolved. I have found that four to six weeks is the time frame to change habit patterns of the mind in most cases. The chimp isn't about to settle into its box if your habit is to dominantly think through this part of the mind.

Hypnosis is the power of language and language creates the metaphoric world in our minds eye. Language creates our fantasy world and language sustains it. Language is what we need to employ to change it.

Your narrative is your self-suggestion; continually going on day after day. It is self-hypnosis. If the instruction you give to your mind is fearful, the mind will construct everything you need to be afraid of, your limbic system, the chimp, jumps out of its box and starts to self-sabotage. What you are holding in your mind it will manifest in reality.

Repetition is the mother of skill. Repetition creates subconscious habits both in action and thinking. Once we have developed a habit it becomes automatic. It is no longer conscious. The brilliance of the mind and also the problem with it. The subconscious can't tell the difference between a good habit and a bad habit. It becomes a perfect servant of what you are training it to do. All athletes train their bodies to do certain things through repetition. How many train their minds to think a certain way?

Not many. When the conscious mind kicks in negatively, it will affect the subconscious processing and the muscle memory that relies on this processing. I often call this paralysis by over analysis. Trust forms when over analysis ceases and focus is on the end goal. Self-hypnosis or self-suggestion needs to be part of the training to bring the mind and body into one focused entity, habitually unperturbed by outside influences. We have the most amazing machine we call a body and the most amazing computer we call the mind but we need to synchronize them. They work together in unison; not apart. Perspiration can get us so far, but inspiration comes from a place where the body and subconscious mind work in tandem and our focus on the goal frees the mind for inspiration. Inspiration comes in a form of possibilities the subconscious mind brings up. If your mind is filled with 'what ifs' it is hard to see what can be. If your mind is looking at probabilities it is hard to see possibilities. To see possibilities you are inspired to find more.

If we look at the Bushido code as a code of ethics. If the actions follow this code there is no problem with doubt and over analysing. It is black and white. The human conscious mind and its computer over-rides the chimp because of the programs running faster than the chimp. The action without thinking based on habitual acceptance of structured habitual beliefs becomes the norm. The discipline of practice; of developing habits that free the mind is the process of seeking perfection. As there is no such thing as perfection, it becomes a process of evolving into more. The self-hypnosis employed was to disregard themselves in the service of a master based on principals of integrity and ethics. This was hammered home until nothing else existed but this purpose: An habitual way of thinking and acting. The self-discipline was the management of the narrative and the training in both mind and body.

There is of course books and books that could be and have been written about hypnosis, but that is not what this book is about. There are often barriers in the subconscious that may come from repressed traumas that would require one on one therapy to resolve. I would suggest you seek a professional clinical hypnotherapist if you feel there is something holding you back. The objective here is for you to understand you are conducting your own hypnotic suggestions to your subconscious each and every day. The best place to start to make changes is in your self-talk.

The saying is true because you will become whatever you hold in your mind, both good and bad, negative and positive, success and failure. It's a choice! Sometimes we feel we have no choice because we get stuck on the habit of negative thoughts. Surround yourself with people of the same philosophical and positive mindset to succeed. A good coach will help you turn weaknesses to strengths through encouragement and support. A poor coach will only highlight what they perceive as a weakness through criticism, creating doubt in your mind about your abilities.

Taking on the critical suggestions of a poor coach is just the start. It perpetuates itself when you start to make the same suggestions to yourself on a regular basis. They may start the ball rolling but you are the one keeping it rolling. If you are not feeling good about yourself it may be because you are surrounding yourself with the wrong people and buying into their negative view of the world.

The mind will succeed in making you unsuccessful if that's the thoughts you are holding in your mind, and I can speak from experience here.

CHAPTER 9

Understanding Habits, Needs and Negative Emotions

Repetition is the mother of skill, and skill is the result of habit. This is the brilliance of the mind. We teach the subconscious mind to do something and then it does it automatically, without thinking. We train the subconscious and it becomes our perfect servant. Compare a new born child's abilities with your own. Adults walk, talk, get dressed and make coffee without much conscious thought. We might consciously make the decision to do something, but then most of it is done subconsciously through the subconscious mind.

We are taught to do many things in life - riding bikes, using computers, driving cars, playing football or net ball - even how to dress and brush our teeth. But no one teaches us anything about our minds and how we use our amazing minds to create our lives. I find this absolutely strange. We have the most amazing computer in the universe between our ears and no one has taught us how to use it. And to make matters worse, much of the programming is done by others before we have developed a rational logical faculty of mind. The people in charge of this programming usually have absolutely no idea how it works. We develop sporting programs to develop physical fitness and skills, but there is not much around to teach people how the mind works or how to develop mental fitness. Much of this book comes from programs I have used with clients - programs that have proven over the past seventeen years to be effective. But don't take it on face value - test it for yourself!

The way we feel is usually a result of our automatic mental habits of thinking - the way we have trained our brains to see the world. If we understand how our brains are trained then surely we can choose what we train them. First, we need to understand what drives our behaviour.

Our behaviour is like the wheels of a car. The ways we think and act are the front wheels leading forward and the way we feel and our physiology are the back wheels following. The engine driving it all contains our five genetic human needs. Our need for love and connection; for empowerment (a feeling that we are important to people: that we have an influence on our lives); for freedom; for fun; and for survival. Survival isn't normally a problem if we have our health, food, shelter and freedom from harm. Freedom and fun go out of the window when the needs for love, connection and empowerment are not being met. Our needs for love and connection and empowerment are usually met through our relationships with others. I would suggest that over ninety five per cent of our problems are relationship problems – past, present, or lack of. I have found this to be true in my practice as a psychotherapist.

These five needs come in different strengths that create different personalities. The person with a high need for love and connection would usually like to be around others most of the time - a sociable person. The person with a high need for empowerment needs to feel important to others and have an influence over their lives - they usually like their own lives to be organised and structured. Someone with a high need for freedom might like their own space; they don't need to be around others all the time. The person with a high need for fun might like new and interesting things and being spontaneous. The person with a high need for survival would tend to be more cautious and less spontaneous. All these needs in differing strengths create a myriad of differing personalities.

My wife has a high need for love and connection - a very sociable person who likes parties and being around others. I on the other hand have a high need for freedom and fun. I have skydived and taught scuba diving, but these days I tend to meditate, read books and paint. I like my own space. You can see the obvious conflict. My wife likes to be around people most of the time and I like my own space and doing my own thing. We have learned to compromise over the past forty years of being together. But that wasn't always the way. We had some magnificent *take no prisoner* battles in the early days that we were lucky to survive.

> **Most of our destructive negative emotions are based on fear - a fear of lacking**

There are basically two types of emotions: love based emotions and fear based emotions. Most of our destructive negative emotions are based on fear - a fear of lacking. I believe that to understand this is to understand what stops us being happy and succeeding in life.

If we want to find the root of our negative emotions we need to look a little further. To a distortion of these needs – *wants*.

A need is something basic that must be met for us to be happy. A *want* is a feeling of lacking something we don't necessarily need. An example of this might be 'I need healthy food to survive. But I *want* it to be donuts and cakes'. Often our short term wants override our long term needs.

About 2500 years ago a guy called Buddha told us that all life is suffering. This was the first of his *noble truths*. The second noble truth was that all suffering comes from craving. So where does this craving come from? It comes from wanting something different. By wanting something different you are basically telling yourself that you are not happy now; you are lacking something that stops you from being happy in this moment - *now*. Due to this perceived lack you are looking at the world in a fearful way and this in turn releases the physiology of fear - our flight or fight response. The body reacts with a general discharge from the sympathetic nervous system releasing hormones such as adrenaline, cortisol and noradrenaline. These hormones produce uncomfortable sensations in the body that are designed by nature to protect us. They create a craving for relief from the stressor by causing us to run away from or fight the threat; the *flight or fight response*. Once the threat is resolved we go back to our normal state.

This system has worked well in our evolution to protect us from the physical threat of harm from wild animals such as sabre toothed tigers. It is not working so well for us now from an emotional point of view - from a mind conceiving irrational threats, and these irrational threats are wants.

So let's take a look at where these wants arise when looking at the mind of today, and in what way these wants are a distortion of our needs.

We can break down the wants into four basic areas to keep things simple.

Love is not something you can get – only something you can give

---

The want for approval

The want for approval is a distortion of the need for love and connection.

Is it possible to get one person's approval all the time? Not likely! Ask my wife. If I could get her approval all the time it would be fantastic, but

UNDERSTANDING HABITS, NEEDS AND NEGATIVE EMOTIONS

I am not perfect. I have my faults just like everyone else. Could I get everyone's approval? No, not much chance of that happening.

The fear of public speaking has its roots in the want for approval. The fear that people won't approve of the way you look, what you are saying and how you are saying it. What if I look foolish, make mistakes or start to blush or stutter? Better just to say nothing and keep my head down because I fear I will not be approved of.

> **The more you want approval, the more you fear you are lacking it**

Social anxiety (a fear of social interaction with others) has its roots in the want for approval as do many low self-esteem issues. The more you want approval, the more you fear you are lacking it. It is impossible to get one person's approval all the time and it is impossible to get everyone's approval. Let's face it; some people are just not going to like us. It's just a fact of life. And yet we crave for people to say nice things about us and have an aversion to their saying things we don't like. 'If people say nice things about me I will feel loved.' Not really. You will just feel approved of and crave more of the same. *You see, love is not something you can get - it is only something you can give.* When a child is born the parents usually have an overwhelming feeling of love for this innocent little thing. The baby is looking back wondering what the hell these strange looking gushing things are. It's the love the parents feel for the child that makes them feel good - not the love the child gives back.

The more you want approval, the more you must feel you lack it. And your mind sees this lack as a threat.

A fear of not winning for the athlete can be based in this want for approval. If I win people will approve of me. The down side is - *you must feel they won't approve of you if you lose*. Any fear will create a negative mindset and doubt. Any fear will interrupt the flow of information between the subconscious and the muscle memory. Fear brings the conscious mind into play.

The samurai would have no want for approval. Why would they? By following the moral virtues of the bushido code, approval would be accepted as a given. Benevolent people are loved, what they give out comes back. True people of virtuous character are admired and respected. These virtues would create a trust and confidence in oneself.

Anger and frustration have their roots in the want to control

The want for control

The want for control is a distortion of the need for empowerment.

Empowerment is to have an influence over things in your life. This need for empowerment is often distorted into wanting to control things. You can't even control your body as it ages. You can't control another person as most parents find out with regard to their children. Control is just an illusion. It's like a want for certainty, but nothing is certain. Anger and frustration have their roots in the want to control. Let's just take the example of a person not being happy because it's wet, cold and raining outside. You can't control the weather. It just is. Not good or bad. It just is. We create a judgement that it is bad for us by wanting it to be warm and sunny but we can't control the weather. It just is. You might have a preference for something else, but if you can't have an influence over it, what's the point losing your happiness over it? How many times do we get frustrated over things beyond our influence - such as being stuck in traffic? Or when our football team loses, or when we get a flat tyre? When the golf ball won't go where we want it to go, or when others don't behave the way we would like them to? The want for control can be seen in the way some people seek to have power over others. Many wars have been fought because of this want. We try to control nature but we soon learn the lesson. The power of nature is far beyond our control. Volcanos spew forth their ash and lava, and tsunamis, cyclones and hurricanes destroy towns and cities.

Unharnessed aggression comes from the want for control and probably the most destructive fear for the athlete. Anger, frustration, impatience will create problems for any athlete when they surface. The athlete can be frustrated by an opponent or even worse, frustrated by their own actions. The use of performance enhancing drugs comes from the want to control. Any cheating will come from this want. Something that starts out as a want for control can often spiral out of control. A true warrior or athlete would never sacrifice their integrity for the illusion of control.

The samurai would develop their skills in martial arts skills to give more influence over a situation, but their mindset was not about control. Self-control was about harnessing aggression and building character. They didn't want power over others because as the name implies; they are 'those that serve'. By following the virtues of bushido the samurai relinquishes control to moral action.

> **Nothing is permanent – nothing is secure**

The want for security

The want for security is a distortion of the need for survival. How can anything be secure when nothing is permanent? We want security of relationships and yet we all die. No relationship is permanent. Security of assets, income and jobs are not permanent. Money comes and goes. Jobs are lost. Assets rust away or are soon past their use by date. Everything is arising and passing away in a universe where everything is constantly changing and nothing is permanent. Even the sun will exhaust its energy and its light will go out. Nothing for me to worry about though; I won't be around that long because my physical existence is not permanent. Just take a look around and see for yourself. Most of the older cars have already gone and the computer that I type this on has already replaced my old one just a few months ago and it will be replaced in times to come. Everything I see around me in the room where I sit will one day find its way to the tip.

For the athlete: The want for security might come from the want to secure a position in a team, or the security of income that comes from winning. None of these things are secure. Cheating and performance enhancing drugs can also play a part here, a sacrifice of integrity for security.

Again we can see in the mindset of the samurai an acceptance of death as the ultimate service, money and material possessions not valued. The samurai lived everyday with the impermanence of life and things in it. Living his life in each moment and living through the virtues of bushido was of prime importance. Nothing else mattered. A simple life with a simple psychological structure of thinking .A life of equanimity, not good or bad, but a life guided by a code of simple moral principle; without want for anything else.

> **Many addictions are formed by the want to escape**

The want to escape

The want to escape is a distortion of the need for freedom and fun. It usually rears its head because we are stuck in the other wants; approval, control and security. Suicide is the ultimate want to escape. It is the want to escape the current situation or responsibilities in life. You can't escape the ups and downs, or the twists and turns of life. It's a roller coaster ride - not a flat road. Many addictions are formed by the want to escape. People turn to drugs, drink, food or even gambling to escape the way they feel about what is happening, or not happening in their lives. They want to escape not being happy. If you are sitting at work watching the clock, wishing you were somewhere else, this is the want to escape. You have responsibilities and need to work, but you would rather be out playing golf.

You can't escape the responsibilities of living or of being a parent or partner in a relationship. Responsibility is just our ability to respond. It is our ability to make a choice but sometimes we feel there is no other choice but to try to escape the situation - to run away. You can't run away from life. Everything is changing and nothing is permanent. Even a situation where a person has thoughts of suicide is in most cases a situation that will pass and resolve itself if that person stays the course.

The want to escape comes from a feeling of hopelessness. This is the flight part of our *flight or fight* response. When you want to escape, you are not focusing on solutions because, in a mind filled with fear, escape is the only solution. There is nothing wrong with wanting to escape a physical threat, it's our natural instinct. The want to escape an emotional threat is another thing. The needs for freedom and fun are frustrated when we feel disconnected and disempowered. This is when the want to escape usually pops its head up. Why would you want to escape this moment, when this is the only time you really have? The want to escape is the want for something different to what you have now. Drugs, alcohol, food and gambling are just short term escapes. The problems are still there when you get back – and usually with added consequences.

The samurai had no want to escape. They accepted their responsibilities with honour, courage and self-control. There is no doubt about the samurai's dedication their duties. The bushido mindset expects nothing less. There is no fear of death as long as it is with honour and courage. The truth character of the samurai is seen at the point of death, not trying to escape it but to welcome it.

This moment is the only time we really have

If we look at the Buddha's teaching, he talks about the impermanence of things. We cling to the good things and feelings and have an aversion to the things and feelings we don't like. Yet they will all arise and pass away. It is also interesting to note that neurological testing on some Buddhist monks has shown them to be among the happiest people. I find this very interesting as they have virtually no possessions of note. They focus on love and compassion for all living things and let go of craving. They meet their basic human needs through co-operation and contribution.

I am not suggesting we all need to become monks, meditating in caves to be happy. But there are some very basic lessons we can learn, as we walk through this journey of life, that can enrich our lives and make them much more enjoyable. Too often we postpone our happiness until a time when we get something we want. It stops us enjoying the moment now and yet this moment is all we have. The past is gone and the future is yet to arrive. This moment is the only time we really have. All time outside of this moment is psychologically mind created time and it only exists in our minds.

The Samurai were greatly influenced by Zen Buddhism and the impermanence of things. To be in the moment is to be in the mind of no thought. Wants take us out of the moment with the mind darting this way and that, looking for threats. It can't be possible to perform at your highest level with such disturbed mind. To be in the moment we must let go of negative wants and move to positive expectations.

CHAPTER 10

The Formation of Many Beliefs

> *What you believe is what you see*

The old saying *'seeing is believing'* is the wrong way around. What we believe is what we see. So where do much of our beliefs come from? Most of our beliefs about ourselves, our lives and others come from the way others relate to us and the way people communicate with us. Many of these beliefs are formed at an early age long before we have developed a rational and logical mind. Children tend to believe what they are told. They believe in Father Christmas, the Tooth Fairy and the Easter Bunny. If you tell them they are stupid, they will believe that too.

William Glasser's *'choice theory'* and in particular, the habits of communication can give us some insights into the formation of many of our positive and negative beliefs. Glasser's theory of the connecting and disconnecting habits of communication were a revelation to me.

The seven connecting habits are:

Caring, supporting, trusting, encouraging, befriending, listening and negotiating (instead of telling).

The more we support and encourage a child, the more that child will grow. There is no limit to the positive beliefs formed through these connecting habits. Most good parents use these connecting habits without thinking. These are the habits we use with our best friends - the only habits we use on our best friends - which is why we feel connected and empowered by them and like to be around them. But how many times do we withdraw these connecting habits when our children don't behave the way we would like them to? Far too often I'm afraid. What happens when we withdraw these connecting habits? The child feels unloved, unworthy and not approved of. Negative limiting beliefs begin to form or are reinforced.

When people use connecting habits on us we feel connected and empowered. I have also found that when using connecting habits, I meet my own needs for love and connection. It works both ways. When they are used on us as children, we feel loved, approved of and liked. Through this (especially when we are children) we form positive unlimited beliefs about ourselves and others. Our positive self-esteem grows.

I have to admit that my parenting skills were lacking. I also recognise that this was apparent in my skills as a manager of others at work. I see my life as a process of evolution, so I don't expect to be perfect. When the student is ready the teacher will appear. In my case the teacher was William Glasser and what he taught seemed like common sense. But common sense is not that common!

The virtue of politeness and respect from the bushido code will come to mind here, connecting habits are all about politeness and respect for another's feelings. Benevolence and mercy also come to mind. By showing politeness and respect, benevolence and mercy you connect and empower not only yourself, but another. It meets the needs of both.

There are also disconnecting habits, and even the best of parents have used these on their children.

The seven disconnecting habits are:

Criticising, complaining, nagging, blaming, threatening, punishing, bribing.

Even the best of parents will have used these disconnecting habits at some time on their children. A great number of bosses use these disconnecting habits on their staff. It's the way we bully each other. These are the habits we use to control someone (although they only serve to make the other person feel disconnected and disempowered). The interesting thing about these habits is that the person using them must feel disconnected and disempowered to be using them in the first place. How disconnected and disempowered must an athlete feel when these habits are used on them, by a coach, trainer or manager? How will it affect their self-esteem? This I have found in practice, to be the greatest influence on an athlete's confidence and self-esteem in a negative way. This is control psychology and it will often backfire. You can't control an athlete, but you can influence them in a positive way using the connecting habits. Disconnecting habits are the way we psychologically bully others.

This is the withdrawal of the bushido virtues of politeness, respect, benevolence and mercy. This is bullying for your own self interests. The samurai has no self-interests but to serve. Disconnecting habits would have been seen for what they are; a lack of self-control and inferior character.

Bullies feel disconnected and disempowered

These habits are like a double edged sword. Disconnecting habits cut the person they are used on and cut the user. What we can see emerging from this is that want for control we discussed before. The more you want control the more you feel you lack it. Disconnecting habits usually come from a place of anger or frustration. Use these habits on a child and they will feel unloved, unworthy and not liked. Tell a child he is stupid often enough and the child will start to believe it. And what we believe is what we see. A child might have the same brain as Albert Einstein but they no longer use it. We tend to take the disconnecting habits personally without realising that it isn't personal. It's the other person who has the problem because they want to control us.

> *You can manage resources but you lead people*

We can see these connecting and disconnecting habits at work in many area, families, business and sports. They are also evident in our parenting style at home, for example, or in a child's interaction with others at school - or in how we communicate with others in sporting teams or in the workforce. But let's use the example of this in the workforce. For want of a better description, we will call the different styles of managers lead managers, and boss managers. You see, you can manage resources but you lead people.

Lead Managers, Coaches and Trainers

Lead Managers will connect with and empower staff through positive feedback and connecting habits. They see mistakes as opportunities to learn; they build morale and know the team creates the results. Staff will enjoy coming to work. They are creative and take less time off. They feel they belong to a team. Most will feel an obligation to work hard and do well and focus on their work and solutions. Lead Managers create a culture of positive expectation. This is like putting money in the bank. You create a surplus. You will eventually gain interest on this investment that will be returned to you in kind. Lead Managers have an influence on people.

When we put this into the sporting arena, the managers become the coaches and trainers. Lead coaches and trainers reinforce the positive self-esteem in athletes, the positive beliefs. There are no limits to the positive beliefs we can have about ourselves.

When we look at the samurai we see they are the moral fabric that binds society through politeness and respect. There is no doubt that there will be times when a coach may need be firm in his feedback to an athlete who is not performing at their best, but this should be presented as feedback with guidance to improve and not direct criticism. It makes all the difference in the world with regard to how it will affect the athletes self-esteem.

Boss Managers, Coaches and Trainers

Boss Managers disconnect and disempower staff through negative feedback or disconnecting habits or no feedback at all. (When talking about boss managers I am talking about the bossy people that use these disconnecting habits all the time on subordinates thinking they are controlling them.) They see mistakes as opportunities to blame. They destroy morale. They think that they are the ones that get the results. Staff don't enjoy being around a boss manager. Many don't enjoy going to work and they gossip and complain behind the boss's back. They take more time off work. This results in people being afraid to make mistakes, and so stops creativity. People are not focused on work but on problems with their boss. It creates a culture of fear and stress. This is like taking money out of the bank. You create a deficit and you will have to pay interest on this deficit at some time in the future. The loss of efficiency and even the loss of good employees will result. You can't fully control another, it's false economy.

In sport the bossy coach or trainer can strip an athlete of their self-esteem, confidence and belief in their abilities. They can also destroy team morale. Many athletes that have come to me for sport psychology, be it basketball players or footballers have been performing well and then go backwards, often it is a new bossy coach that is the culprit and this is the first place to look. It's fair to say that some people handle criticism better than others. Some people like to use the term 'constructive criticism', but it is rarely constructive if it demotivates an athlete rather than motivates. Constructive feedback, highlighting the positives and offering solutions to the negatives is a better way to go.

An athlete usually knows when they are not performing at their best. They need solutions, not a focus on problems. We need to reinforce positive self-esteem and beliefs, not tap into the negative.

Looking at the Bushido code you will notice politeness and respect as a virtue, benevolence and mercy, honesty and sincerity. I don't think anyone using disconnecting habits on someone is being polite and respectful. They are just trying to control another person.

We can now start to understand the formation of our positive and negative belief system - how our self-esteem is affected through our relationships with others. We start to develop some irrational fears - the wants for approval, control and security - and the world becomes a scary place to live.

I did feel some guilt, regret and disappointment over my own communications skills with my children once I understood the habits of communication. We were never taught how to be parents at school. We usually did what was done to us. And even the best of parents have used disconnecting habits to try to control their children. I see the subconscious mind like an amazing computer that is being programmed by people such as parents, with absolutely no idea what they are doing. Luckily, we can reprogram it, and once reprogramed, it becomes a perfect servant. Disconnecting habits are all about control but we can never really control another person. But we can have an influence over people by the use of connecting habits.

Guilt is one of the most ridiculous emotions we can foster

Parents often use guilt as a method of control, but guilt is one of the most ridiculous emotions we can foster. Guilt offers a lesson and nothing more. You rob a bank, feel guilty, give the money back and never rob another bank. The guilt has served its purpose. I soon got over the guilt in my parenting skills and took the lesson to heart.

THE FORMATION OR MANY BELIEFS

I wonder just how often you use disconnecting habits on yourself in your own negative self-talk and how guilty you make yourself feel. We often take over where others left off. You can become your own biggest critic, feeding your own negative self-esteem and negative belief system. You have to be careful about what you keep suggesting to yourself. *Your continued suggestions will become your beliefs and what you believe you will see.*

Negative self-talk in sport only creates anger and frustration. This is the biggest barrier to developing a winning mindset. It creates doubt and doubt is based in fear.

> **The new car or bigger house should be the by-product of a happy life, not the reason for it**

To simplify the belief system I will take an approach that many in psychological circles might not agree with, but I believe in simplifying things.

I group the non-limiting beliefs into the category of the true self - our positive self-esteem. The negative limiting beliefs I refer to, for simplicity, as the ego - our negative self-esteem. I see the ego as a protection mechanism that has developed to protect us from emotional pain, because much of it was created through the emotional pain we felt as a child. When the child thought it was a victim of something or someone, it sought approval, control and security; all the things it felt it lacked at that time in its life. The ego wants us to feel superior, but in the wanting of it, it makes us feel inferior. If we have the approval of others we feel superior. If we have control or power over others we feel superior. If we get money and possessions we feel secure and superior. Any want that is satisfied will soon be replaced by another want - and so the suffering of craving follows us - never satisfied. Don't get me wrong here; there is nothing wrong with having a preference for the new car or bigger house but, it should be a by-product of a happy life, not the reason for it.

If you want sweet plums you don't plant the seeds of a bitter lemon

If you want sweet plums you don't plant the seeds of a bitter lemon. What seeds are you planting?

The character of the samurai was created from the seeds of bushido; A code of chivalrous virtue based on sound psychological principles. These principles are as true today as they were then. Any athlete seen as noble and having integrity is a role model to others. The athlete who is polite and respectful will be respected. This type of athlete will be calm of mind and focused. They will have a presence of undisturbed power and self-control.

CHAPTER 11

How the Mind Works

Our imagination fills in the gaps of perception

Imagination

Imagination

The subconscious can't tell the difference between a real or imagined experience. Researchers at Harvard University tested people practicing playing five notes on a piano over a week. Neural activity in the frontal cortex of the brain started spreading like dandelions spreading across a field. They had the same results from a second group that just imagined playing the notes on the piano for a week. The imagination should be used as a tool of creation. Only see what you would like to create, not what you don't want to create. The subconscious doesn't discern between good or bad. It delivers what you are holding in your mind. Your conscious mind sets the goal and the subconscious delivers it.

We create through our imagination, so what are we creating? So many people create drama in their lives because that's what they imagine through a system of wanting. They see a lack in their lives and are left lacking. What is wrong with seeing this world as a world of adventure and comedy? It is a choice, but the habit patterns of the mind, looking for threats and wants, make it see drama, and so create drama. Do you imagine a fearful world? All too often we don't see the imagination as a tool of creation. Many tools can be dangerous if we don't use them properly.

We often say our imagination runs wild but we can harness it to create the things we would like to bring into our lives. This is where we have choice. *The only thing that stops us believing we have no choice is that we are sometimes stuck in the habit of wanting.*

Any athlete who has achieved great things saw it first in their imagination. Our imagination creates our future. If we imagine it often enough we come to believe it's true. The subconscious can't tell the difference between a real or imagined experience. Every athlete at the pinnacle of their sport, imagined it long before they got there. When we say someone has vision we are really just saying they are using their imagination and moving towards something.

What is coming in through the senses is information. The eyes are like cameras, the ears like microphones, taste and smell are just chemical receptors, the skin like a mass of pressure and heat sensors. The body is an information gathering machine. We take this information and try to give it meaning, and this is where we have a choice. We have a choice how we focus our minds. In our minds, we are often filling in the gaps in sensory information through our imagination to give it meaning. An example of this could be seeing two people whispering, and imagining that they are talking about you. We can choose to focus our mind in a negative way or a positive way. But often the front wheels of the car (the way we think and act) are stuck in a rut, focusing on wants.

Positive imagery and self-talk can have a great impact on an athlete's ability, both from an improved performance point of view and from a healing point of view after injury. These things are now scientifically proven and should be incorporated as part of an athlete's training. Positive imagery and self-talk reinforce positive beliefs.

> ***The positive unlimited beliefs tap into the true self and the negative limiting beliefs form our protection mechanism, the Ego***

Beliefs

Many of our beliefs are created by the way people relate to us, especially when we are children. Do these beliefs of the ego work for us or do they create problems for us? Sadly the negative beliefs strip us of our ability to be happy and to achieve what we would like to bring into our lives. These beliefs are not you. You were not born with them and they are nothing more than irrational fears. The positive unlimited beliefs tap into the true self and the negative limiting beliefs form our protection mechanism, the Ego.

> ***We are often so afraid to fail that sometimes we won't even try***

Our own negative self-talk, and the use of disconnecting habits on ourselves, feeds negative beliefs. They continue to grow, self-sabotaging our abilities and achievements. What you believe you will see. And if you believe you will fail, guess what? You will fail. We are often so afraid to fail that sometimes we won't even try. As a child did you fail to walk when you fell after taking that first step; or fell off your bike when you first learned to ride it? You didn't fail: you were learning all the time. Making mistakes is how we learn. We are not perfect - we are in a process of evolving. We are evolving through the mistakes we make, and mistakes are a natural part of our learning process. The belief system becomes a filter in the way we see the world and what we believe we see.

For an athlete, belief is all important. If you believe you can, you can. If you believe you can't you cant. It is beliefs working at a subconscious level that manifest our reality. Positive beliefs are the absence of negative wants and the creation of a positive expectations.

The Bushido code is designed to develop a set of moral beliefs. These moral beliefs are the foundation on which all else sits and create a strong base of personal integrity and character. From this base the mind is free from wants, indecision or doubt and action will flow with purpose and intent.

Conscious focus is a choice

To start to train the mind we have to understand that we have a choice in the way we focus our creative ability and reclaim our ability to choose. This can be difficult at first. The negative habits of the mind are habits and the ego is a protection mechanism. The ego doesn't want to relinquish control. If it relinquishes control, how will you be protected? Protected from what? From irrational emotional wants that can never be satisfied? The ego tells us we have a right to be afraid, a right to be upset and a right to be angry. It can be very determined in this. It knows from past experience that we didn't always get what we wanted.

The problem with choosing to change is the habit patterns of the mind. As I mentioned earlier, I liken this to driving down the road on the left hand side in Australia without even thinking about it. Try driving down the right hand side in America and see how uncomfortable it can be. It takes us out of our comfort zone and our comfort zone is the limit of our positive beliefs. So it will be uncomfortable when we first start making these changes - and that's fine. As you expand your comfort zone you are growing and evolving. Our lives should be a continuous process of expanding and evolving. But all too often we find our comfort zones shrinking or contracting.

There isn't a habit stronger than the mind that created it. Athletes often work to change bad habits in their skill sets to develop good habits. Not many athletes work on changing bad habits in their mindset. To change mindset you need to reclaim your power of choice from habitual thinking. Eventually the new mindset will become a habit.

Shifting your focus from wants to expectations

How do we change the mind from wanting? This should be the question you are asking yourself by now. Well, this shift is subtle. If we look at a want as a fear of lacking something, we can see it is pessimistic, rigid, fearful and focusing on problems. The subtle change is to turn this want into an expectation. Expectations are more optimistic, flexible and focus on solutions. Expectations must be realistic expectations. If they are unrealistic they are just wants disguised as expectation.

> *A want is never satisfied until we get what we want*

Let's take a look at what has become known as the Stockdale paradox. Vice Admiral James Bond Stockdale (December 23, 1923 – July 5, 2005) was one of the most highly decorated officers in the history of the United States Navy.

Stockdale, while Commander of Carrier Air Wing 16 aboard the carrier USS *Oriskany*, was shot down over enemy territory on September 9, 1965. Stockdale was the highest-ranking naval officer held as a prisoner of war in Vietnam. Stockdale was held as a prisoner of war in the Hoa Lo prison for over seven years.

In a business book by James C. Collins called *Good to Great*, Collins writes about a conversation he had with Stockdale regarding his coping strategy during his period in the Vietnamese POW camp.

'I never lost faith in the end of the story, I never doubted not only that I would get out, but also that I would prevail in the end and turn the experience into the defining event of my life, which, in retrospect, I would not trade.'

When Collins asked who didn't make it out of Vietnam, Stockdale replied:

'Oh, that's easy, the optimists. Oh, they were the ones who said, 'We're going to be out by Christmas.' And Christmas would come, and Christmas would go. Then they'd say, 'We're going to be out by Easter.' And Easter would come, and Easter would go. And then Thanksgiving, and then it would be Christmas again. And they died of a broken heart.'

Stockdale then added:

This is a very important lesson. You must never confuse faith that you will prevail in the end—which you can never afford to lose—with the discipline to confront the most brutal facts of your current reality, whatever they might be'.

I think Stockdale was also an optimist but with a realist attitude. He expected a favorable outcome as all optimists do, but this was tempered with a realist attitude of not wanting it, but expecting it. The optimists Stockdale was talking about were those stuck in wanting. Their expectations were unrealistic and therefore wants.

Now you can see that a want is never satisfied until we get what we want. It's a subtle change in the way we think that creates a big difference in the way we feel. We rob ourselves of our happiness with these little irritations, when it really doesn't matter at all.

When we focus on wants we change our physiology to one of fear. And we have developed a terrific defence mechanism to deal with fear - our flight or fight response. This defence mechanism was fantastic to protect us from wild animals, but not so good when the threat is an irrational emotional fear. The release of adrenaline, noradrenaline and cortisol create uncomfortable feelings in the body. These sensations are designed through evolution to be uncomfortable. This discomfort creates a craving for relief from the threat. In the past we ran away and hid in caves, felt safe and went back to our normal state. Or we picked up a spear, killed or fought off the threat, felt safe and went back to our normal state. This defence mechanism has served us well over time and is one of the reasons we are on top of the food chain. It doesn't serve us well when it comes to irrational emotional fears created through the ego - the fear of lacking something. These emotional fears release the same uncomfortable hormones as they did in response to a physical threat - just as a meerkat stands on its back legs, head darting this way and that looking for physical threats. Our minds also dart this way and that, looking for and finding emotional threats that are not rational or logical.

For the athlete, the wants will usually bring frustration, anger and unharnessed aggression. This will usually interfere with the subconscious communications with the body and trained muscle memory - the conscious mind getting in the way of subconscious processing.

> *The ego is just a programmed version of looking at the world in a threatening way through a filter of negative beliefs*

Negative focus

Now we might be starting to understand this defence mechanism, this ego, and we might be beginning to understand it isn't us. It's just a programmed version of looking at the world in a threatening way through a filter of negative beliefs. Much of it is created through the use of disconnecting habits and the withdrawal of connecting habits. - habits that we then turn on ourselves and continue to feed by our own negative self-talk. This then becomes out narrative.

We can now see that when we focus on the want for approval, control and security, we are saying that we fear - we are lacking something. The mind now sees the future in a fearful way and we begin to feel anxious. Or we might go back to the past with regret, disappointment and guilt and feel down and depressed. We often skip between the two - between anxiety and depression. How could we possibly be happy with this frame of mind? By recognising it is only a frame of mind, a perception, *not reality* - just our perception of reality - just an illusion we create.

> **What I am holding in my mind I am bringing into my world by the way I think and act**

Positive focus

If we change our mind to rational, logical realistic expectations we are moving away from wants. It is just a change in focus and self-talk. Over time this will become habitual. We will then be opening the mind to possibilities and opportunities we can take advantage of.

If we chose to imagine that people are saying bad things about us we will usually act in a way that brings it about. If we chose to imagine that people are saying good things about us we will usually act in a way that brings it about. The reality may be that they are not talking about us at all. How many time do we assume the worst only to find out we were wrong. There is no doubt that there will be time that people are saying negative things about us, but that is coming from their judgements and beliefs.

I have a friend who asked me why so many people fear public speaking when he enjoyed it. I told him that he thought everyone liked him. He said 'well I suppose I do, I'm a nice enough guy'. I said 'not everyone will like you.' He said 'well that's their problem, not mine.' He had a positive expectation but it was realistic. He didn't want everyone's approval.

Gamblers typically have unrealistic expectation. The odds are against them, the house always wins in the end. It is set up that way. The odd few that win lotto or a big win on the slot machines are the exception that fuel this unrealistic expectation. They just fuel the wants in others to the benefit of the house. Realistic expectations must agree with logic.

Our positive focus on realistic expectations must be tested against logic to avoid faulty reasoning.

> *The subconscious can't tell the difference between a real or imagined experience*

Physiology of stress

Acknowledging how our minds affect the way we feel is to realise how our thinking creates changes in our physiology. We can also start to see what the Buddha was talking about 2500 years ago when he said that all of life is suffering and all suffering comes from craving. The craving comes from the intense desire for relief from the uncomfortable chemicals we release in the body when seeing the world in a fearful way - from an ego point of view. Aggression, anxiety and depression are mind created stressful states that strip us of our happiness. Let's face it; we are not going to be releasing serotonin and dopamine, (the feel good chemicals), if there is a sabre tooth tiger coming at us. We would be patting it on the head instead of running away! The flight or fight response works perfectly for real physical threats but is not so good for imagined emotional threats.

> *Suppressed emotional issues will find their way out one way or another*

If we look at our Immune system we see it is designed to fight threats at a cellular level. Autoimmune diseases arise from an overactive immune response of the body against substances and tissues normally present in the body. In other words, the immune system mistakes some part of the body as a pathogen (a threat) and attacks its own cells. We know that continued stress will affect out health in a negative way. Could the cause of this be the body turning back on its self because we feel powerless to resolve an emotional issue or trauma – the suppression of this resulting in the body attacking itself? *Suppressed emotional issues will find their way out one way or another.*

> *Nothing is permanent and all things must pass*

Nothing is permanent and all things must pass. Why get attached to something that is not permanent? But we do. We cling to the good feelings and have an aversion to the bad feelings. As we cling to the good feelings they soon disappear and our aversion to the bad feelings only perpetuates them but none of them are permanent. When we look at thoughts and feelings with equanimity, we are withdrawing the judgement of good or bad. This in turn stops the mind from seeing the threat and that in turn changes the body's chemistry.

Are you feeding the good wolf or the bad wolf?

Here is a story I heard or read a number of years ago. I believe it puts the ego and true self in a nutshell. It is about a wise old American Indian chief giving advice to his grandson. The chief says to his grandson.

'Grandson, there are two wolves inside us all, a good wolf, and a bad wolf, and they are fighting all the time. The good wolf is love and compassion, courage, generosity, fortitude, discipline, laughter and every worthy virtue a human being is capable of. The bad wolf is anger, hatred, laziness, jealousy, envy, greed, sloth and other vices a human being is capable of.

The grandson looked at the old chief and said. 'But grandfather, if they are fighting, which one wins?'

'The one you feed is the one that wins,' said the wise old chief.

Which one are you feeding?

Our life experiences can cause us to doubt our ideals and our basic moral beliefs when we feel like a victim. It's not hard to see how some experiences might feed the "bad wolf". For many of us it might seem easier to feed the bad wolf, giving in to negative wants and giving up on virtue. To do so is to become a victim of yourself. To lose your moral compass is to lose yourself to fear.

The Bushido code was designed to starve the bad wolf and feed the good wolf. The psychology of fear can't be fed from a point of moral virtue. To feed the bad wolf is to feed the fear.

What do you need to do now that you know this? You can choose the way you think and what you focus on. You can shift from wants to realistic expectations. Let your feelings be your guide. If you are feeling down, upset, angry or frustrated; change your mind. If you don't mind it won't matter. This really is mind over matter.

MINDSET OF THE WARRIOR

CHAPTER 12

The Mind is a Time Machine

> *There is no time but NOW!*

If we were in possession of a time machine, we wouldn't go back to the worst past we could think of or forward to the most frightening future, but isn't that just what we continually do with the mind? We think back to the past with regret, disappointment and guilt. Then we think of the future with a want for approval, control or security – all the time seeing life in a fearful way. Looking at the past this way makes us depressed and looking at the future this way makes us anxious. We are not living in the present. And yet the present is the only time we really have. All else is just an imagination or a memory and can we really trust our memories?

If the subconscious can't tell the difference between a real or imagined experience, how do we know if memory is real or imagined? Our strongest memories are usually attached to strong emotional feelings at the time. These can be both positive and negative emotions. We know through the work of Bandler and Grinder in NLP that we can reframe memories. We don't get rid of them but we can change them. No two people experience something the same way, so no two people have the same memories of the same event.

If we are feeling emotional down about something and recall a past similar experience, we often amplify the emotion attached to the past experience - *Changing it*.

Sometimes we can reminisce about a number of past experiences and begin to blend them into the same experience – *Distorting it*.

If we can change memories and distort them how can we truly know what was true?

The point I am making is not to discredit memory but to understand it is malleable. A person beaten in the past would know they have been beaten, but their perception of it would be different to the perpetrators. The reliving of it may also attach more to it than what was there in the first place.

I began to realise that the subconscious can't tell the difference between a real or imagined experience. Portions of my own past have been coloured by my imagination and can't be trusted.

There is also a condition called false memory syndrome. This comes about when for example, it is implied to a person that they may have been abused in the past. This creates an imagination of the possible abuse which can in turn create a false memory of the imagined event.

Depression often has its roots in the distorted past

What is the point of continually going over negative memories with regret, disappointment and guilt when our version of the event might be an amplified distortion far worse than the event itself? If it was bad enough the first time, why continue to relive it over and over again in this time machine of the mind? The past can only serve to offer lessons and should be left behind so we can live in the 'now'. Depression often has its roots in the distorted past. There are some people in the world with full recall of all the days in their lives from around ten to fourteen years of age, but these are rare exceptions. The rest of us might have perfect memories locked away in our subconscious but the recall can be tainted, coloured, or even imagined.

Our imagination is our creative faculty. It's a tool, but do we usually use it as a tool? We can use this tool to imagine what we would like to bring into our life and then come back to this moment and do the things we need to do now to bring it to fruition. If you look around at all the man-made things in your surroundings, you will see how someone's imagination was at work as a creative faculty. All the things you see were at one time only in someone's imagination. We often use this imagination to worry about the future, thinking of the worst things that could happen. We kick in the want for approval, control and security and see the world as a fearful place, and most of the things people worry about never happen. What a waste of this wonderful creative ability!

Athletes often focus on the last loss with regret, disappointment and guilt. They continue to beat themselves up using disconnecting habits long after the event. All this will do is strip them of their confidence. It is already past and you can't get it back. If there is a lesson to be learned then learn it and leave the past behind. If you don't, it will be like baggage weighing you down in the future. A negative focus on the past will tend to create more wants and fears in the present.

What to do with this information? Understand your thought system is not you. It is a tool that we use to create. Learn to harness its potential to create a happier life and not let it run around like a bull in a china shop. Thoughts just bubble up in the mind but you don't have to listen to them. Turn your wants into expectations and dismiss or ignore the negative thoughts.

Anxiety has its roots in the imagined future - stuck in the wants for approval, control and security. Depression will often have its roots in the past with regret disappointment and guilt.

The Bushido code is designed to have the Samurai live in the moment. There is no regret, disappointment or guilt about past actions because they come from a point of virtue and service. All actions in the present come from the same moral code to create the future.

It reminds me of the 'Stockdale paradox' mentioned earlier. Stockdale endured many years as a prisoner of war. His belief was that you must retain the faith that you will prevail in the end regardless of difficulties, while at the same time, confront the brutal facts of your current reality whatever they may be.

This can be true for the athlete retaining their faith that they will prevail in the end – even with their current reality of past failures.

Stockdale had faith in his expectation of freedom with the acceptance of what was, and without the attachment to a time frame of wants.

CHAPTER 13

Our Judgements become Filters

Our judgements become filters of perception

When we make a judgement we are saying this is good for me or bad for me - we are polarising our opinion. One example of this could be the weather. On a cold, wet and windy day someone might say they hate this type of weather. It's just weather, not good or bad, it just is. The judgement is a want for something different, but you can't control the weather. How many people give away their happiness by wanting to control something like the weather - something that is beyond their control? The judgement that this is bad for us creates the want. We might have a preference for something different but a judgement that cold, wet rainy days are bad will create a lot of unhappy days in our lives. Nature has a way of bringing these days into our lives when we want them least - as often happens when I plan to play golf!

Many judgements are made to the effect that something is good or bad - black or white. We no longer see all shades of grey. We create a filter of perception and the mind starts looking for everything that agrees with the filter and disregards the rest. We can see that filter at work for some people with regard to the weather. And isn't it interesting that we often call it bad weather?

If we withhold judgement we open up our perception to see all shades of grey. We are more likely to see reality than our limited, filtered view of it. Many judgements become beliefs and what we believe we will see.

The more judgemental we are the more we close down other possibilities

Our judgements create filters of perception just as our beliefs create filters of perception. The more judgemental we are the more we close down other possibilities.

How many athletes are already making strong judgements about their opponent's perceived abilities before an event? Often amplifying their opponents strengths and minimising their weaknesses. They are also often minimising their own strengths and amplifying their own weaknesses through their judgements.

Withdraw judgement to see possibilities

Our thinking system becomes our representation of the world we see. Just as a map of Australia represent the territory of Australia. But the map is not the territory, just a representation of the territory.

There are things we do in our thinking system to make it more efficient.

We can distort the present to see what we would like to bring into our world in the future, through or imagination. It's how we create.

We delete most of the information coming in through the senses, because we would be overwhelmed with all the information if we didn't. We choose what's important to us. We generalise things like doors, front doors, back doors, glass doors, cupboard doors etc. to make our communication more efficient.

When we delete, distort and generalise through negative filtered judgements and beliefs - we begin to create an impoverished representation of our world.

Racist beliefs are nothing more than generalisations. If you generalise your judgements or beliefs on race or religion, the world you see is not the world of reality. Just a limited view of a created reality. You see an impoverished world of fear.

Deleting positives to focus on negatives will also create an impoverished world. We often forget to be grateful for what we have and focus on what we have not. Our wants. An old saying comes to mind *'I was unhappy I had no shoes, until I saw a man who had no feet.'*

Distorting things is usually about distorting things to fit our beliefs and judgements. People often distort things to blame others. Any lie is just a distortion of reality. How many athletes buy into a distorted reality by thinking that a loss is the worst thing that has ever happened to them. It could be the best thing that ever happened to them if they can get a valuable lesson from it.

Every athlete will have to endure a loss. It's not bad or good, it just is. You can bury yourself in the negative generalisations, distortions and deletions but it won't help. This is the ego's domain. What is the lesson you need to learn from it? Train harder, change mindset, change strategy, develop new skills? Learn from it and then drop it. *You can learn more from a loss than a win, if you withdraw your judgements about it.*

What can you do about this? You can withdraw the judgement of the situation or the person. Accept and allow the situation as neither good nor bad, it just is. You might have a preference for something else, but accept it and allow it to be just as it is, letting go of wanting to change it.

Then look to see what possibilities can come from this. An example might be the judgement about the end of a bad relationship. You might look at the possibility of now finding a good relationship. We will look at a technique to let go in a later chapter.

People are judgemental, it is our nature to judge people and situations. But do our judgements empower us or disempower us. Are they generalisations, distortions or deletions tailored to suit a limiting and impoverished mindset? We will never see good in a person if we have already judged them as bad.

When we look at the bushido mindset of the samurai, we can see the virtues as a way to eliminate generalisations, distortions and deletions. Anyone coming from a moral and ethical code of conduct has a representational system free of fear. Although this code of conduct can seem judgemental and black and white in itself - it is based on the sound psychological principles of contribution and cooperation that meet our needs.

The UFC fighter who has generalised, distorted and deleted their reality about a skill set, may think they can't strike, wrestle or grapple. They wouldn't be a professional UFC fighter if they couldn't do all three. They may be stronger in one area but must possess skills in all areas to be accepted into the UFC.

CHAPTER 14

The Essence of what we are

Try to find yourself. Am I this hand that I see before me typing on the keys? It looks like my hand; it has my wedding ring on it and my short stubby fingers. But am I these hands? Can I feel the wetness of the blood running through the fingers or the individual bones and muscles? No. Can I feel the finger nails or know the length of the fingers without looking at them? No. Can I feel where the skin stops and the air begins? No. I can feel some sort of vibration, but without looking at that hand I may as well have a hoof on the end of it. So where am I?

What about the heart? I can have a heart transplant and still be here. What about the brain? It can be damaged and I am still here. Some people have had half their brain removed and they are still here. It must be the feelings then. But most are just electro-chemical reactions caused by thoughts. I must be getting closer. The thoughts - but I was here before I learned a language which is the basis of this thought system - so I can't be thoughts. So I can't be found in the body, the feelings, thoughts - so where am I, because I know I am here?

The way to find out what is behind thoughts is to stop them. How do you stop them? Try watching for the next thought to pop up in your mind. Did you notice the thoughts stop as you became the observer of them? So what is this observer?

> **The observer must be pure consciousness, pure awareness**

So the essence of what I am must be this formless consciousness. You can slice and dice the body into the smallest parts and you won't find it because it is beyond form. It is formless which is why it is so hard to find. It can only be experienced - like love. It's like emptiness or a 'nothingness', filled with whatever we are aware of.

There are two things that can't be stressed. You can't stress nothing, because there is nothing to stress, and you can't stress everything. By definition, if it contains everything, there is nothing left to stress it. So the essence of what we are is stress free - until we break things down into individual things and judge these things as good for us or bad for us - creating a filter of perception. What's coming in through the senses is just information light waves, sound waves etc. It's just information in our awareness until we colour it through the filter of the belief/judgement system to give it meaning.

Now this is where things get interesting. If it is not in our awareness, it doesn't exist for us at that point in time. Let's take this a step further. I go to sleep at night and my awareness of this physical universe closes down; it no longer exists. I am blissfully unaware of anything going on around me. I wake in the morning and my senses again become aware of the physical universe. So here is the crunch, if this physical universe only exists for me when I am aware of it, I must be the centre of my own universe. The physical universe only exists for me, through my conscious awareness of it. If I am the centre of my own universe I must be the creator of it, and in co-creation with all the other billions of universes on this planet earth. If I am not here consciously, this physical universe can no longer exist for me. If one million people died in an earthquake on the other side of the planet, I would not be affected by it until I saw the news or read a paper. It would not be a part of my reality, not in my awareness.

The universe will continue to unfold through its own grand design and through the law of cause and effect, everything arising and passing away, evolving. But we still have a creative impact in our own little universe as we arise and pass away because we are also a part of this elegant design and are creative in our own right. We humans are evolving. Charles Darwin said that it was not the strongest or most intelligent of the species that evolves the best, but the most adaptable. We have used our intelligence to adapt to even the most inhospitable environments. In this way we are creative.

So what are you creating? Is it drama? What you believe is what you will see. If you wake up in the morning and see a world of drama, that's just what you will create through a filter system of beliefs and judgements. What is wrong with seeing the world and life as an adventure, a comedy, a loving place to be? This difference in perception is a world of difference in emotional experience.

Take a look at your life as though it is a movie

Take a look at your life as though it is a movie - a movie with you as the main actor, director and producer. What type of movie would you like to create? A magnificent love story? Then see it as a love story and go out and create it. Like any movie it will have its twists and turns, its ups and downs; but life is a roller coaster. Are you too afraid to get on the roller coaster -sitting with envy while watching others having so much fun? On the first incline of the roller coaster we tend to feel apprehension. Wouldn't it be better to be back safe on the ground? Why did I do this? My apprehension might be building. This tends to turn to exhilaration once over the first incline when I realise there was nothing to fear but the fear itself. I see the people getting off the roller coaster with faces full of excitement, vibrant and full of energy.

I also see the people with fear in their eyes, too afraid to get onto the roller coaster ride. I like to see life as an adventure and a comedy. I laugh at the golf ball that heads off into the trees never to be found, (and believe me, this happens often in my game). I hit a little ball around a field. What's the point in getting upset at something that isn't really important for me in the scheme of things?

A professional golfer asked me to caddy for him during a Pro Am. He was experiencing difficulty with anger and frustration - the want for control. On the first hole he stuffed up a shot and went one over par. By the fifth hole he was four over par and was getting more frustrated with every hole. I told him on the fifth that he had carried that first bad shot on his back for the last four holes. I asked him when he was going to put it down and let it go. I said he was four over, wasn't going to win, so he might as well just enjoy the day out. 'This is your psychological advice?' he asked.

'Yes, just let it go and enjoy the game.' I told him. He went three under par for the remainder of the game.'

'You just don't care do you?' is what he said to me on the way home.

I said, 'No, I am carefree but that doesn't mean I care less. I just don't take most things too seriously. You cared too much about that first bad shot and held onto it.'

> *Sometimes we need to just take off our heads and live through our hearts and just be in the moment*

Judgements and beliefs stop us seeing reality and enjoying the moment. To enjoy the moment and experience the essence of what we are, we need to get out of our heads and away from the *paralysis of over analysis*. Accept what is, clear the mind of judgements and you will find peace.

What can you do to create a happier life and be more successful in your sport? You can first accept that you are the creator of it. See your life the way you would like it to be and then live it that way. What you are holding in your mind you will bring into your world.

I can recall a conversation with UFC fighter George Sotiropolis when he was without fear or doubt in a couple of his fights. His mind drifted to fancying a pizza, and wondering what his wife was busy with, while he was in the middle of the fight. He said it was a surreal experience. There was no attachment to winning or losing - to technique. His mind was free to wander as the subconscious and muscle memory did was it does best.

We are not about to suggest you go into your next competition thinking about pizzas. A fixation on anything will create a problem. It is to understand that a mind free of attachment flows and is unrestricted.

From the point of view from the bushido code. The virtues are designed to avoid paralysis by over analysis. To free the mind to be in the moment, the only time we have. All martial artist masters from the past have promoted the mind of no mind. Free to flow from situation to situation like water passing around rocks in a stream. To free the subconscious from the interruption of decision. Decision and choice is something that can only come from a conscious perspective. The less you are trained in skills and technique, the more your conscious mind will want to intervene. The more you are trained in skills and technique, the less you will think about it and your skills and technique will flow.

CHAPTER 15

We all Live in an Illusion

Imagine sitting still in a valley on the stump of a chopped down tree, with the roots still deep in the earth creating a solid foundation. It is just before dawn. The night is quiet and you are waiting for the sun to rise in the sky. Across the valley is the silhouette of a mountain in front of a night sky covered in bright twinkling stars.

The first hint of red appears behind a mountain and the lower stars begin to fade as the sun begins to rise. An orange glow forms behind the mountain and the birds come alive with their dawn chorus. There is glow of light over the mountain as the sun begins to rise, turning the sky from black to blue. The stars begin to fade from view and the shadow of the mountain retreats across the valley like a swarm of ants running from the light. The sun continues to rise until it is high above the valley and the valley is full of life.

Now let us take a look at reality.

Nothing in the universe is still

Go back until just before dawn. Place your imagination into the tree stump - into the roots gripping the soil and boulders below. Then place your imagination into the earth itself - this magnificent Earth hurtling through space on its orbit around the sun. It is travelling at over 100,000 kilometres per hour. Imagine you can feel the large mass of the Earth hurtling through space with incredible accuracy. It rotates on its axis and you are sitting on its surface travelling at 1670 kilometres per hour if you are on the equator. As you look across the sky, you see the mountain moving across the starry night sky, as the large mass of the Earth rotates on its axis with such power and precision while hurtling through space. It's rotating to a point where the sun's rays hit the atmosphere above, turning the sky red then orange and obscuring the stars from view. There is a glow of light as the mountain begins to move across the face of the sun while the Earth rotates on its axis. Small particles in the atmosphere scatter the light and turn the sky blue - the stars fade from view. Birds wake and the shadows recede across the valley as the Earth continues to revolve on its axis. The mind is under the illusion that we are sitting still and the sun is rising. Nothing is still. Even the atoms in a stone are travelling faster than we can comprehend.

Imagine now looking at the Earth from a place out in space - the blue greens of the sea and the greens, browns and yellows of the land. Swirling white clouds and snow covered polar caps and mountains rotate slowly on the Earth's axis while it all hurtles through space. Imagine the dark side with tiny lights around the coastline highlighting the darkness of the sea, sparkling like a diamond necklace in the night.

Imagine the Earth half bathed in darkness and half bathed in light. See this Earth revolving out of darkness and into light, and out of light into darkness. Can you see time? Can you see yesterday or tomorrow? Even time is just an illusion created in the mind. Zoom in until you are over a city watching people like ants rushing back and forth so earnestly, taking everything so seriously. How small are our lives in the scheme of things? How insignificant. Everything in this magnificent universe arises and passes away as it continues to evolve. Nothing permanent and nothing still. This universe is evolving through the universal laws of cause and effect; of chaos and stability; and in patterns that no longer seem random. Such an elegant design - evolution based on universal laws that don't discriminate. The butterfly effect from the chaos theory suggests that a butterfly flapping its wings in Australia will eventually have an effect on weather patterns in New York. In turn, each choice you make will lead to a different future - even the smallest choice. Billions of people make billions of choices creating a myriad of possible futures - all interconnected. Each choice is a cause that will have an effect on the future.

A quark is an elementary particle and a fundamental constituent of matter. Quarks combine to form composite particles called hadrons, the most stable of which are protons and neutrons - the components of atomic nuclei. This computer I type on has more space between the atoms than the atoms themselves. The more we look at matter, the more we see the illusion of it. There is more space than particles, and every particle broken down is more space and less matter, yet, I type on this computer under the illusion that it's solid matter. It is just energy vibrating at different frequencies creating the illusion of something solid. We think we can comprehend this world through our limited senses but we have no idea. My dog runs to the door when my son's car enters the bottom of the street. He must hear and know the sound of the car. I can't hear it or recognise it, but I know he is coming. My dog tells me so. If I go to meditate in my bedroom, that same dog will seek me out and sit by my side throughout the meditation. I have no idea how he knows or why he comes at this time – but he is there without fail; and if I lock the door he will scratch to get in. There are many things we can't comprehend, yet still we know through experience. There are many things we can comprehend and yet still live with an illusion of something different because of our habits of thinking - our conditioning.

Everything is borrowed then left behind

Most choices we make come from the illusion that we require approval, control or security to be happy. It's an impossible illusion to satisfy - nice to have but impossible to get. Another Illusion is that we own anything. Everything is borrowed and left behind. My car, my house, my wife, my children and my money are not mine – none is permanent. All one day will be left behind. All that we really leave behind is our influence on others. A kind word and a smile is your legacy. This will remain long after your house has fallen to bits and your car has rusted itself out of existence.

The ego thinks in terms of the little me, the little mine, the little I. The ego is under the illusion that it is you, and we are often under the illusion that *it is* us. It is the ego that hides reality behind an illusion of often irrational and illogical limiting beliefs. Then life becomes all about me, what's mine and I need more. Where can I find me in this body with thoughts and feelings that are impermanent, continually arising and passing away? There is no permanent me! What could ever possibly be really mine when I enter this world with nothing and leave with the same? Who am I? A psychotherapist, father, grandfather or husband - I can find myself in any of these situations - they are just roles I play. The ego latches itself onto this - I, me and mine - like a parasite latching onto a host.

There are things we can't perceive through our limited senses, but we know them to be true because we experience them. I can switch on a light and see the effect of electricity but I can't see the electricity. My mobile phone rings and I am soon speaking to a friend who could be on the other side of the world. I talk to George on skype but I have no idea how it works. I can't see the radio waves or even know how they can get through the walls and windows. I just know that they exist because I experience them. Science looks to find ways to harness the elegant design of this universe of energy for our benefit. We may not understand or need to understand the science, but we can see the truth of it in our experience.

Our emotional experience of life is often something we don't understand. We tend to look outside for its cause. This is the illusion created by the ego. All we emotionally experience is mind created. Everything outside is just information coming in through the senses. It's how we chose to perceive this information that creates the emotional feelings. The cause is our perception and the effect is our feelings. This is the point where the great illusion begins and is the domain of the ego.

The ego likes to blame everything and everyone outside of us for our suffering. The Dalai Lama came to Australia a few years ago. The Prime Minister and the leader of the opposition had still not agreed to meet with him because of pressure from the Chinese government. When asked what he thought about this he said, 'I will be happy if they would like to meet with me and I will be happy if they don't.' The Dalai Lama was not about to let his happiness be affected by something he had no influence over. There was no want for control or approval - no illusion - just an acceptance of what was true. He didn't take it personally. There was no effect on his feelings.

What can you do with this information? You can see the wants for what they are, an illusionary fear. And what is this fear? I came across this definition, **F**alse **E**vidence **A**ppearing **R**eal.

The bushido code of conduct sees life as impermanent ,death is not feared but embraced as a part of life. There is no illusion in its virtues. They meet their needs and the needs of others through cooperation and contribution. A virtuous life is considered all that is important. The samurai are just cells in an organism called a community, playing their part. When we see the Japanese people endure a recent devastating tsunami with such acceptance and dignity, we can understand how deep the bushido code is still a part of this remarkable culture. I was amazed at their resilience but more important, their dignity and humility.

There is no doubt that Japan in some areas of military persuasion lost their focus on virtue when the gun replaced the sword. But this must have been a hard choice for many. The sword can't fight the gun. An unskilled gunman can still kill the greatest swordsman. Chivalry was lost with the gun. The bushido code was not lost on all the Japanese though - it is still evident today. It is still a part of their culture and we could see it in action when Japan was ravaged by a Tsunami. The dignity, acceptance and strength displayed could only come from a point of virtue and mindset.

CHAPTER 16

The Root of all Craving

All craving comes from wants

I was once told that 50,000 thoughts are bubbling up in a person's mind each day and many of these thoughts are the same thoughts. I don't know how anyone managed to count them but the figure is irrelevant. We have thoughts bubbling up into our consciousness on a continuing basis. The thoughts are meaningless until we make a judgement about them and create a want. Wet, cold weather is the example we turn to again. Weather is not good or bad unless the mind perceives it as so. We have positive and negative thoughts arising and passing away. When we attach ourselves to a thought, we perpetuate it and strengthen it by thinking about it. We give it energy.

The ego wants us to be a victim

Positive and negative thoughts bubble up. They have no real impact upon the way we feel until we start thinking about them. If we make a negative judgement we create a want for something different - we fear we are lacking something. This fear releases adrenaline, noradrenaline and cortisol as a fear response to a threat thus creating uncomfortable feelings. These feelings perpetuate more thoughts as the mind continues to try to resolve a threat which in turn perpetuates more feelings. The cycle of the thought/feeling system creates a craving for relief. This cycle can turn anxiety into panic attacks or frustration into anger. It can overwhelm us. Now we can understand Buddha's statement that all of life is suffering and all suffering comes from craving. Stuck in our heads we go off to the future with a want for control, approval and security - thus creating anxiety. Or off we go to the past with regret, disappointment and guilt - creating depression. We are not living in the moment and the ego tells us we have every right to feel depressed. This is the stubbornness of the ego and the resistance to letting go. The ego wants us to be a victim - only as a victim can it survive. Its role is to protect us from being a victim, so we need to be a victim to require its protection. It was created from a victim mentality and much of it was formed prior to the development of a rational logical mind. The mind of a child is like a sponge. It is vulnerable to soaking up negative comments and taking them personally. What might seem a fair punishment for an adult, will often be seen as a personal attack by a child who has yet to develop a fully rational and logical mind.

> *It is the reaction, with a liking or disliking, craving or an aversion, that creates our suffering - our craving for more or less*

The sense organs are lifeless unless the conscious mind comes into contact with them. The function of the conscious mind is just to know without differentiating. Then the next part of the mind starts working – perception or human consciousness. Our judgement of good or bad is based on memories of past experience. Next, the third part of the mind starts working with the creation of sensations. The judgement that it is good for us will create pleasant sensations and the judgement that it is bad for us will create unpleasant sensations. These sensations arise in the body and are felt by the mind. The fourth part of the mind now begins to work - reaction. Someone says something nice to us and the pleasant sensations arise. We like them and crave more. Someone says something nasty to us and we create unpleasant sensations and we start disliking them. We have an aversion to them and crave freedom from them. It is the reaction, with a liking or disliking, craving or an aversion, that creates our suffering - our craving for more or less.

What about thinking through the heart? Now you might question how you can think through the heart. It is less about thinking and more an instinctive feeling that can precede the thoughts and balance the mind to postpone reacting negatively. This is also not about the physical heart but the essence of being in the moment, this moment *now*, with allowance and acceptance and a positive expectation. Realistic expectations are positive, flexible and focus on a solution. Wants are negative, rigid and focus on a problem. Looking at people through the heart, the feelings precede the thoughts if we are in the habit of feeling love and compassion for others. This can be more an instinctive process developed through understanding. Through the head the thoughts precede the feelings. Now a little story to get a greater understanding of how it works.

We have an office car park for clients. There are signs to let people know it is a private car park. We are across from a hospital that has a public carpark that charges people to park. I personally don't think it is ethical for people to be charge exorbitant prices to see their sick or injured family and friends, but it is the way of the world today.

One day a man parked his car in our carpark taking the last carpark and proceeded to walk across to the hospital. I told him there was parking at the hospital and that this parking was reserved for our clients. After a torrid of abuse and some physical threats, he marched off shouting to me to get the car towed away, he didn't care.

Most people would take this personal but is it? He would have reacted to anyone who questioned his right to park there. Funny how his right to park without paying overrides my clients rights to free parking in his eyes. They should pay so he doesn't have to?

Of course there was a bit of adrenaline firing up in the system, but a simple instruction to the mind changed that. 'Poor man' I thought. Who knows why he was angry, maybe he is like that all the time, feeling a victim of life. Maybe his wife is dying in hospital or his son has been in a car crash. I don't know why he is suffering but I do know he is or he wouldn't react that way.

The thought or instruction 'Poor man' would trigger compassion. The mind looks for all the reasons to feel sorry for him. Compassion is a form of love, and the thinking moves us to the heart and an acceptance of what is.

It is a bit like the young terrorist who is conditioned into thinking he must die for his God. Funny how the people giving religious conditioning don't seem in any rush to do the same most of the time. Most older men are too wise in the ways of the world to buy into it. That is unless they get a feeling of power from it. That is just the want to control being satisfied. If martyrdom is such a great thing, Why are we not all dancing towards the edge of the cliff like lemmings. I feel compassion for those who feel compelled to give their lives for conditioned beliefs installed by others. Life is for living. I also feel more compassion for the victims of their senseless actions. We will find many times in our life when we come across people being made victims, sacrificed for the wants of others. We are far from being fully evolved as a species. Consciousness is a double edged sword. It is new in the evolutionary process. Let's just hope we don't destroy ourselves in the process. The last dinosaurs of man will not give up easily, they will fight to the death in order to survive. We can see this in every dictatorship around the world. They don't hesitate to kill in the fight for survival, but all eventually fall or die. They leave with nothing.

THE ROOT OF ALL CRAVING

I am not religious but many good stories in religious texts can show us the truth of how we should think. Christ on the cross. 'Forgive them lord for they know not what they do'. Whether any god hears this or not, it is the instruction to the mind that would give peace to Christ. This acceptance and allowance of the differences in peoples beliefs is to see reality. Humans are not perfect nor is the world we live in. I like to think I am perfectly imperfect, That way I get to enjoy my imperfections. I am sure my wife wouldn't agree with this though. I think some of my imperfections cause her great frustration, but that's what makes us human and our marriage might be boring without it. Just as her imperfections are a great joy to me. My wife's imperfections allow me to accept mine. This is what makes her perfect in every way to me.

Just in case my wife ever reads this book. It is about sport psychologically and she has no interest in the subject so she will probably not bother and that is fine with me. I must say that I do love her imperfections. Well, most of them as she does mine. Most of them but maybe not all, and that's OK.

> **There are many things a man can take to appease his tortured pallet, but it won't appease his tortured soul**

So how do we break this cycle of reaction? The next chapter will answer that.

The bushido code of conduct is based on virtues. The mind that doesn't waver from these virtues is at peace and free from cravings. Its basis is in Buddhist teachings which is all about letting go of cravings. Buddhist philosophy is the foundation of bushido. A mind trained to be at peace and living in the moment. In this book I am trying to give this understanding from a modern day view of psychology and the basic wants that create the daily cravings we feel. I am not claiming to be an enlightened being free from wants, this is just part of the evolutionary process. We are all just evolving. We are not perfect and we accept that. Knowledge comes in three stages. 1) We can be told something. 2)

Intellectually we can understand it. 3) True knowledge only comes when we experience it.

It is an ongoing process of evolution to move from the second stage to the third and develop these habits of thinking. The old reptilian, mammalian brain always wants to pull us back to our animalistic roots and a mind of fear. The ego doesn't want to lose its place in our life and keeps bringing up this illusion of emotional threats .It does get weaker over time though as the new habits of thinking kick in.

CHAPTER 17

How to Release Negative Emotions

> *If you are not releasing negative emotions - you are suppressing them*

The thought/feeling system is a circular system that feeds itself. The thoughts feed the feelings and in turn the feelings feed the thoughts. Or looked at another way, the thoughts create the sensations we feel and the sensations we feel perpetuate the thoughts. The sensations create a craving for relief and the mind looks for relief through the flight or fight response. Frustration can develop into anger and anxiety that can develop into panic attacks through this feedback system. Just like the feedback of an amplifier that continually gets louder and louder deafening the ears or, in this case, overwhelming the mind. We can create an uncomfortable rage or an overwhelming fear through this feedback system. We must realise that the brilliance of the subconscious mind is its ability to learn through the development of habits, but the subconscious mind is not discerning about the habits we create. It can create good habits as well as bad. It is our reaction to the sensations that must be the point at which we begin to work. The judgement or perception of something as being good or bad for us creates the want and with the want comes the craving for relief.

We might now look now at the Buddha's Awareness Meditation - becoming aware of the sensations arising and passing away in the body and looking at these sensations with equanimity. They are not good or bad - just sensations that arise and pass away. Some are unpleasant sensations and some are pleasant - but none are permanent. If they are not permanent they are not me, not I, not mine. We cling to the pleasant sensations and have an aversion to the unpleasant sensations - a craving for more or a craving for less. Now I am not so sure about you, but I have a family to support. I can't head off into a cave to practise meditating on this for the next seven years - but I can learn a lot from this that allows me to be much happier now. The Awareness Meditation is about acceptance and allowance to break the cycle of reaction and craving. If we look at the root cause of our negative emotions coming from the want for approval, control and security, then we can use this as a starting point to learn to release and let go of these negative emotions.

Many of our problems come from the suppression of these negative emotions. It's like adding skins to an onion; the onion grows. The universal law of cause and effect would indicate that if we plant bitter seeds, at some time in the future we will have to harvest a bitter crop. The wants are the bitter seeds that grow to create a bitter harvest in our lives. Learning to release and let go of the negative emotions is like peeling back the skins of the onion. At its centre we begin to realise that there is nothing to fear but the fear itself.

So how do we release and let go of these wants? We must release our attachment to them before we can let them go. What are we attached to? We are attached to being the victim: attached to our judgements, that become filters. It is the ego's attachment born from being a victim and perpetuated through victim mentality. So we become a victim of our ego-self, and the ego is like a scavenger dog. It is always scavenging for something or someone else to blame for the way we feel. The ego is a protection mechanism which requires us to be a victim for its survival. But it's the ego, not us - just a conditioned response.

> **It is okay to have thoughts and feelings. This isn't good or bad - it just is**

We must bring a problem into our awareness if it isn't already there. We will make a judgement about this as being bad for us and creating a want for something different - a craving for relief. The first step is to allow those thoughts and feelings to be there by telling yourself, 'It is okay to have these thoughts and feelings. This isn't good or bad - it just is.' Here we are trying to withdraw judgement and accept what is. We might have a preference for something else, but at this point we are looking at an acceptance and allowance of what is in this moment: the withdrawal of the judgement about it. You might at this point want to look at the problem. The threat: is it a want of approval, control or security? It might be all three, such as in the case of jealousy. You don't really need to know what want it is to get an acceptance and allowance of it, and to tell yourself, 'it is okay to feel this way'. Through allowing and accepting the thoughts and feelings we are telling the mind that this is not a threat. If your mind stops seeing it as a threat, you stop releasing the adrenaline, noradrenaline and cortisol that create those uncomfortable sensations. We break the thinking/feeling feedback cycle of reaction. Now we need to relax into these feelings with an allowance and acceptance. It is okay to relax into an allowance and acceptance of these thoughts and feelings and just let them be. As in meditation, we are moving to a point of looking at the thoughts and feelings with equanimity, without judgement - not good or bad for us - they just are. Where in meditations we are looking at all sensations, with this method we are working on specific problems creating the thoughts and sensations and our judgements about them. You can of course use it just to focus on the feelings. Can I find myself in any of these thoughts and feelings? You will find you can't find yourself in any of these thoughts and feelings. Can I just let them go or do I want to remain a victim of them? Why would you want to remain a victim of your own thoughts and feelings? Can I accept them as they are without judgement and then let them go? Yes. Will I accept them as they are and then let them go? Yes. When? Give yourself permission, say 'Now'. Then just withdraw the judgement about them and relax into an acceptance and allowance of them. I often find it beneficial to say now with a sigh as I breathe out and relax into them. In this process we are giving the mind permission to let go of the attachment to wanting. For some, the feelings can be like a stress ball in the stomach area. I used to imagine the ball dissolve as I let go. It could be butterflies that disperse, or just breathing out a black cloud of negativity. Use your imagination to find the way that works best for you. You want to be able to disperse or dissolve the feelings in some way. The idea behind this is to develop a habit through repetition of its use. I don't need to think of the process now, it has become a habit of letting go over the years. The process develops the habit and the habit becomes automatic.

This technique is not much different to what the Buddha taught in awareness meditation, looking at the feelings with equanimity. Not good or bad. Giving permission to accept and allow them to be, and not seeing them as a threat. The process is similar to a part of the 'Sedona Method' developed by Lester Levenson, and taught by Hale Dwoskin. The Sedona method takes you through a number of processes to release emotions and you can find out more at: www.sedona.com. I found the program to be very practical, beneficial and recommend it. Like any process, it can be adapted to suit yourself. I have adapted it to help my clients and hopefully help you. It is nothing new, it has been around in different forms for 2,500 years. We are just supplying a modern day version based on modern psychology. We are all standing on the shoulders of the people that went before.

The process to release

Get on touch with the thoughts and feelings of something that bothers you and say to yourself.

I don't want to change this.

It is okay to have these thoughts and feelings. This isn't good or bad. It just is.

It is okay to feel this way.

It is okay to relax into an allowance and acceptance of these thoughts and feelings without judgement, and just let them be, just as they are.

Can I find myself in any of these thoughts and feelings?

Can I just let them go, or do I want to remain a victim of them?

Can I accept them for what they are, without judgement and then let them go? Yes.

Will I accept them for what they are and then let them go? Yes.

When? Now…………..

This process might sound simplistic but often the simple things are most effective. Practised often enough the process becomes a habit. All that I have left of the process is an internal sigh as I breathe out. I no longer need to go through the full process and I often find I have released automatically without doing anything. I supply a CD to my clients that they listen to each day to establish the technique and develop the habit of letting things go. I find the CDs are effective therapy - a cheap and effective way to have a therapy session each day without me even being there. An MP3 of the technique using clinical hypnotherapy to get the mind more suggestive can be downloaded from my website at: www.melbournehypnosis.net.au.

We often find ourselves swimming against the current of life

Many people worry about things they have no control over. Does this serve any purpose? No. The vast majority of the things we worry about never eventuate, but we get stuck with an attachment to the problem. We get stuck wanting something different - feeling we are lacking something that stops us being happy. Look back at all the things you worried about a month ago and you will see what I mean. It was a waste of time and energy. You always get by - you always get through. Stuck in negative thinking it is often hard to see a solution. Sometimes there is no solution other than to let go and just go with the flow. We often find ourselves swimming against the current of life, feeling as though we are drowning in it. Even if we are successful swimming against the current we will only find smaller rivers and streams. Eventually we end up on the rocks. When we learn to go with the flow, we drift into an ocean of good feelings. Learning to release negative emotions is learning to go with the ebb and flow of life.

The bushido code of virtues develops the mind through a number of virtues. With this installed as a way of seeing the world, especially at an early age, the negative emotions wouldn't arise. The problems we have in modern day society is that the mind is conditioned to look for threats, not conditioned to be fearless. To be fearless the samurai would need a strong psychological foundation and this is where the bushido code of virtues comes in.

CHAPTER 18

Our Suffering creates our Motivation to Change

> *One choice can change our future and every choice will*

The Buddha in his first *noble truth* said that all of life is suffering. We don't like to suffer but we do suffer. Let's take a look at Chaos Theory to understand the need to suffer.

Chaos Theory studies the behaviour of dynamic or open systems that are highly sensitive to initial conditions. A *dynamic or open system* is a system which continuously interacts with, and is influenced by, its environment. Human beings are a dynamic or open system that can be vastly influenced by small changes in conditions. This chaos theory effect is popularly referred to as the *butterfly* effect. The name of the effect was coined by Edward Lorenz, a meteorologist. It is derived from the example that states that a small thing, such as a butterfly flapping its wings, can create a ripple effect that could have an influence in the creation of a hurricane several weeks later. It was discovered that even the smallest changes will have an impact on future weather conditions. There are a number of movies that use this theory to base different outcomes on different choices – leading to many different conclusions. I like this theory. It suits my stronger needs for freedom and fun. *One choice can change our future: and every choice will.* Our future is created by the choices we make now. We are the creators of our future – creators in our own right.

The Chaos Theory suggests that an open system will continually change and develop to a point of turbulence before transforming into something stable. Out of chaos comes order.

We can see this in evolution. It is the organisms that adapt best to changing environmental instability that survive. The instability creates suffering and the suffering creates a requirement to adapt and change - to evolve. If you don't adapt and evolve you don't survive. Just ask the dinosaurs. We don't really know why they became extinct but we can be fairly sure it was because they couldn't adapt to changing conditions. (The only thing I know about dinosaurs is that they had big feet, were supposed to generally have had small brains, and that I wouldn't have wanted to be following one around the back garden with a pooper scooper!)

It is suggested by science that the earth is 4.5 billion years old. 2.5 million years ago the Genus Homo appeared. 200,000 years ago man started looking much like he does today and 25,000 years ago Neanderthal man became extinct. Physically, we have not evolved much in 200,000 years. However, we have evolved consciously over a relatively brief period. Julian Jayne suggests in his book, *The Origin of Consciousness in the Breakdown of the Bicameral Mind*, that human consciousness as we know it is fairly new and was a leap in our evolution over a short period of time. Jayne suggests that human consciousness did not begin far back in animal evolution. It is a learned process brought into being out of an earlier hallucinatory mentality by cataclysm and catastrophe only 3000 years ago and is still developing.

OUR SUFFERING CREATES OR MOTIVATION TO CHANGE

It's interesting to note that many religions use the same time frame for God breathing life into the creation of man.

With this leap we became self-conscious and this was probably the beginning of the development of the ego. Because of this leap in consciousness, I now sit typing on this computer and receive emails from half way around the world in the blink of an eye. I turn on a tap and water pours out, flick a switch and the room lights up. Humans are masters at adapting - but still we suffer. We know the body won't evolve during the course of our lifetime (although mine seems to be evolving into a wrinkled, slightly balding, saggy version of what it once was), but the mind can evolve and adapt. Maybe those enlightened souls of the past were examples of the next step in the evolutionary ladder. Christ said, 'You too can do these things.' The Buddha called it the eradication of suffering, which must be the pinnacle of evolution. I find this an interesting concept. All that is, God if you like, becoming aware of itself through human consciousness. Still, it is just a concept. I am not enlightened enough to know if it's true or not. We can take this concept to its extreme. Suppose we all become enlightened, and eradicate all our cravings; would we still want sex? Let's face it, you don't hear much about those enlightened beings from the past having kids after becoming enlightened. Without babies the human race would cease to exist. We would become extinct. Interesting thought: extinct if we don't adapt and possibly extinct if we reach the pinnacle of adaptation. Probably not - there can be great joy and love in sexual union; it can be much deeper than satisfying the basic sexual urge we are genetically disposed to for procreation.

> **We see so much anxiety and depression in the world today but often don't see this as an opportunity to evolve**

So a leap in consciousness may have been brought about through suffering and our ability to adapt. Suffering in this context would indicate that it creates the motivation to change, to evolve. We see so much anxiety and depression in the world today but often don't see this as an opportunity to evolve. A pill is prescribed and popped like a band aid, covering the root cause of the problem which, in most cases is our thinking. No one teaches us how to think - how to use this amazing computer as a tool for positive creation. And it is a tool. We didn't have this thinking system until we learned a language. And the development of analogy and metaphor to expand language created a different thinking system. It is not us. It is a learned tool.

> **Stuck in our thoughts, and looking at the world in a fearful way, we create our own suffering**

But we have become addicted to popping pills to make us feel better and relieve the suffering we feel. Irvin Kirsch is a professor of psychology and specialist on the placebo effect. He is also author of the book, *The Emperor's New Drugs*. Drug companies claims that the effectiveness of antidepressants has been proven in published clinical trials showing the drugs worked significantly better than placebos. He suggests that a closer look at the data shows that the difference between the drug response and the placebo response is not that great. That many of the effects of antidepressants seem to be due to the placebo effect. What is the placebo? A placebo is nothing more than a sugar pill that works on the belief system. If you believe you will feel better - you will. Back to what we believe we will see. This belief system is so powerful.

So, our suffering can be the catalyst that brings about our transformation like a caterpillar turning into a butterfly. From chaos comes order. I don't know about you but I don't like the idea of changing my brain chemistry with a pill. There will obviously be cases when this is required due to a deficiency in the system - the body not working the way it should. If the mind isn't working the way it should then, in most cases (though not all), if we change the mind we resolve the problem. But we have become a society looking for a quick fix and instant gratification.

OUR SUFFERING CREATES OR MOTIVATION TO CHANGE

If we take the example of the suffering an athlete can feel after a loss. This disturbance can come from regret, disappointment and guilt which in turn can create depression. There are also the feelings that they will not be approved of by their supporters and the want for security of the winning prize, which to a professional athlete with be the prize money, sponsorship options, their income. Both wants will create anxiety. A focus on this will strip an athlete of their confidence and self-esteem. Some athletes take the baggage from a loss into their next competition. This is where you see them perform without passion or choke just as they are about to succeed. Choking comes from changing a winning mindset into a wanting mindset. An athlete can be quick to embrace their wins but unwilling to embrace their losses. Losses are part of the game. It's a fact of competition that someone will win and someone will lose. If you can't embrace your loss you won't learn anything from it. You can learn more from a loss than you ever will from a win. Use the suffering created from a loss to learn something from it. What do you need to change? The answers will be there - they must be. Learn from them and leave it behind.

If we look at our suffering as the chaos required, that creates the motivation to change and adapt, then we can see it for the gem that it is. Out of the muddied pond the lotus flower rises and blossoms.

What can you do with this information? Embrace your suffering and see it as an opportunity and motivation for change - an opportunity to evolve.

From the athletes point of view. The suffering can come from a series of losses that disturb the mindset. Some might lose confidence or motivation, some might even give up altogether .Others will use it as a motivation to change something To train harder, learn new skills and adapt. The right mindset is required to make the right choices and to see the opportunity – and it takes courage to let things go.

Without the right mindset we will perpetuate the suffering through irrational wants. It is easy to blame someone or something else for our problem but it won't fix it. You can't fix a problem with the same mind that created it.

If we look at this in the concept of the bushido code. The training of the mind in the virtues of bushido eradicates the suffering that comes from wants and doubts. It is a process that evolves the mind from a strong psychological standpoint and foundation, that creates a platform for all thoughts and actions. The mind is unperturbed by the ebb and flow of life's trivialities and challenges. All thoughts and actions are grounded in the virtues of bushido. The instructions to the mind and actions become habits: subconscious habits. This frees the mind to be in the moment.

CHAPTER 19

Purpose, Sociopaths, Integrity and Ethics

Getting back to the bushido code of conduct:

Rectitude or justice

Rectitude can be described as morally correct thinking and behaviour - Integrity; honesty; righteousness; straightforwardness. This is considered the strongest virtue of the bushido code, the virtue on which all others rest. This is the corner stone of bushido. Rectitude is the power to decide on a course of action in accordance with reason. The corner stone in rational and logical behaviour must have its basics in how we think.

We can now see how the basis of a superior mindset is based in purpose, integrity and ethics. So this must be the foundation on which to build an immovable mindset. Without this foundation the building is weak.

How can the mind be balanced and clear without a clear moral code of conduct? We would be continually questioning ourselves. What is the boundary, what is the limit? Without clear boundary's; don't children push the limits?

Once you exceed your boundaries you have lost your moral compass in whatever you do. You have lost you belief in what is right or wrong. The virtues of bushido are telling you what is right and wrong, based on what is good for you and what is good for all that come in contact with you. It is a code of ethics designed to create ethical behaviour that develops integrity.

Understand yourself and understand others

Purpose

Philosophers have pondered over the meaning of life for thousands of years - the purpose of it all. Am I here to claim to know the meaning of life? Well, not exactly. It's more about the meaning of our needs - the purpose behind our needs. If our needs drive our behaviour, there must be an evolutionary purpose in the development of them. William Glasser, a psychiatrist and developer of reality therapy and choice theory, came up with the theory of these basic needs, and the habits of communication. When we look at them they make sense and are simple to understand. If we understand the purpose of our needs we can see the purpose behind the evolution of them.

Let's now look at these needs again - the needs for love and connection, empowerment, freedom, fun and survival. We can see that our needs are more complex than the needs of other animals. This could be the reason why we are at the top of the food chain. The complexity of our needs could have been the catalyst for our leap to a higher level of consciousness - a conscious choice as opposed to just basic animal instincts to survive. With conscious choice comes responsibility. Some don't like the sound of that, but *responsibility is just the ability to respond – the ability to make a choice.*

PURPOSE, SOCIOPATHS, INTEGRITY AND ETHICS

Survival is the basis of all needs - every living thing has this basic need. Many mammals developed the need for love and belonging. They suckled their young and many of them banded together in groups for protection. This gave mammals an increased level of survival. Then the need for power came in. We can see this in the animal world, with stags banging heads together, and silver-backed gorillas banging their chests (not much different to the way some people behave today). The strong and powerful also dominated the mating game and had a better chance of surviving and creating more offspring and strengthening the gene pool. Human beings then developed into a different species to anything else. We could now choose how to think. Of course the strong were still dominating and so freedom entered as a need - the freedom from the power of others - to be free from their domination in order to survive. For the more advanced consciously, I suggest the need for power was being tempered by a need for empowerment. This is more about recognition and having an influence over one's life than power over others. A high need for power over others conflicts with the needs for love, connection and belonging. It frustrates this need. The need for fun - to experience new things, to learn new things - also developed from basic play. The more we learned; the more love, connection, empowerment and freedom we could get and the better were our chances of survival and the survival of the human race.

Human beings began to spread across the world in conquest of others, or for freedom from others. Some were still driven by the base need for power - others shifting to empowerment. These set up groups that were more co-operative and democratic. Let's face it - that's what being human is all about. These needs have developed to bring human beings together in co-operation and contribution for the benefit and continued propagation and survival of the species.

It's a bit like a cell in the body. The cell's co-operation and contribution to the whole perpetuates life in the body. If it takes more than it gives, it becomes cancerous and threatens the life of the body. The purpose of our needs is simple and based in the need for survival – co-operation and contribution to the whole. If we look at our purpose, it is co-operation and contribution first to family and friends, then to the broader community, and then to the whole of society. The purpose of business is to provide a positive service to society and in doing so, be paid for this service. The basic purpose of government is to make sure all people have food, shelter and freedom from harm - to provide systems of health care and education, and to protect the environment for future generations. The problems we see in society today all around the world comes from the failure of governments, businesses and individuals to recognise our true purpose. It often takes something like a devastating tsunami to wake people up to the need to help those less fortunate - to begin to feel love and compassion for our fellow man - to change our focus from what I can get, to what I can give. The ego is all about getting.

We have a responsibility to meet our needs and, in so doing so, we meet the needs of others. If we are living for a purpose of co-operation and contribution, we can't help but meet our needs. So what stops us living with this purpose and meeting our needs? Thinking we can't be happy because we lack something, and this creates a want for more - more money, more possessions, more approval, more control, more security.

What is integrity of a system? There is a box of tissues on my desk. The system has integrity if it holds the tissues in place and allows me access to the tissues, one at a time. It serves the purpose for which it was designed. What if the bottom dropped out of the box? The system would lack integrity. It would not serve the purpose for which it was designed. So integrity and purpose go hand in hand.

Sociopaths

There are many psychological disorders that we can come across in society, but there is one in particular that I would like to cover with regard to integrity. Why single out this one? Because we often think people with this disorder are normal and exhibit normal behaviour. I refer to the sociopath. Sociopaths can blend into society, and I have had to work with quite a few over the years. They often leave a trail of destruction behind them and much pain and suffering for others. They feel no remorse, guilt or empathy - they lack integrity. The sociopath has a purely egoist point of view – it is all about them. A sociopath will usually be a bully, but a bully might not be a sociopath. I focus on sociopaths because I see them as extreme form of ego – giving the appearance of control but they are usually out of control. Why? It's because of their high want for control.

Let's take a look at the profile of a sociopath so that we can recognise them when we come into contact with them:
- Glibness and superficial charm
- Manipulative and conning
  Sociopaths never recognize the rights of others and see their self-serving behaviours as permissible. They appear to be charming, yet are covertly hostile and domineering, seeing their victim as merely an instrument to be used. They may dominate and humiliate their victims.
- Grandiose sense of self
  Feels entitled to certain things as *their right*.
- Pathological lying
  Sociopaths have no problem lying coolly and easily and it is almost impossible for them to be truthful on a consistent basis. They can create, and get caught up in a complex belief about their own powers and abilities. Extremely convincing and even able to pass lie detector tests.
- Lack of remorse, shame or guilt
  Sociopaths have a deep seated rage, which is split off and

repressed. They do not see others around them as people, but only as targets and opportunities. Instead of friends, they have victims and accomplices who end up as victims. The end always justifies the means and they let nothing stand in their way.

- Shallow emotions
  When sociopaths show what seems to be warmth, joy, love and compassion it is more feigned than genuine and serves an ulterior motive. They are outraged by insignificant matters, yet remain unmoved and cold by what would upset a normal person. Since they are not genuine, neither are their promises.
- Inability to love
- Need for stimulation
  Sociopaths are living on the edge. Verbal outbursts and physical punishments are normal
- Callousness/lack of empathy
  Unable to empathize with the pain of their victims, having only contempt for others' feelings of distress and readily taking advantage of them.
- Poor behavioural controls/impulsive nature
  Rage and abuse, alternating with small expressions of love and approval produce an addictive cycle for abuser and abused, as well as creating hopelessness in the victim. Believe they are all-powerful, all-knowing, entitled to every wish, no sense of personal boundaries and no concern for their impact on others.
- Irresponsibility/unreliability
  Not concerned about wrecking others' lives and dreams. Oblivious or indifferent to the devastation they cause. Do not accept blame themselves, but blame others - even for acts they themselves obviously committed.

Other Related Traits:

Contemptuous of those who seek to understand them. Do not perceive that anything is wrong with them. Authoritarian. Secretive. Paranoid. Only rarely in difficulty with the law, but seek out situations where their tyrannical behaviour will be tolerated, condoned, or admired.
Conventional appearance. Goal of enslavement of their victims. Exercise despotic control over every aspect of a victim's life. Have an emotional need to justify their crimes and therefore need their victim's affirmation

(respect, gratitude and love). Ultimate goal is the creation of a willing victim. Incapable of real human attachment to another. Unable to feel remorse or guilt. Extreme narcissism and grandiosity.

Have you seen these traits in people you have come in contact with? Many sociopaths reach high levels in business and politics. Sociopaths are not interested in co-operation and contribution. It is all about the base need for power and control. They have very little need for love and belonging. It is all about satisfying wants at any cost. The need for power has its roots in the want for control, approval and security. It is good to look at the sociopath. They are all around us creating great destruction. Hitler, Saddam Hussein and Gaddafi are examples. Many politicians are more subtle in their quest for power but still show sociopathic tendencies. Sociopaths seem to be stuck in an evolutionary time warp and lack integrity - the needs of a silver-backed gorilla with the intellect and ego of a human. The sociopath is the domain of the ultimate ego mind.

Integrity

The integrity of the system of contribution and co-operation repairs itself and evolves

The human condition has evolved through the development of our basic needs. These needs have evolved through co-operation and contribution. History has shown that a sociopath's behaviour and the resulting destruction they cause, usually leads to their own self-destruction. Out of chaos comes order. The integrity of the system of contribution and co-operation repairs itself and evolves. Democracy is founded on co-operation and contribution.

So, the integrity of the system of human evolution requires co-operation and contribution. Let's now take this a step further and look at integrity from an ethical point of view. In ethics, integrity is regarded as the honesty and truthfulness or accuracy of one's actions. We can see the sociopath fails when it comes to integrity, but this usually comes back to bite them in one way or another. We can also see the lack of integrity in our political systems and politicians. Even systems that are supposed to be democratic have politicians that lie and manipulate for power. A lie has its roots in the want for control. Deception has its roots in the want for control. Stealing is a want for approval, control and security.

> **To see what others have and what we have not is a temptation to want more - at whatever cost**

Let's take a look at religion as a basis for ethical behaviour. We can look at the Ten Commandments and the Buddha's Eight-fold path for this. I am not religious but there are valid lessons to learn here.

Ethics

Ethics and the Ten Commandments.

We can see that commandments five through to ten have their base in ethics and integrity.

5: Honour your father and your mother.

6: You shall not murder.

7: You shall not commit adultery.

8: You shall not steal.

9: You shall not bear false witness against your neighbour.

PURPOSE, SOCIOPATHS, INTEGRITY AND ETHICS

10: You shall not covet your neighbour's house; you shall not covet your neighbour's wife, nor his male servant, nor his female servant, nor his ox, nor his donkey, nor anything that is your neighbour's.

(I don't know about you but I am certainly not about to covet my neighbours ass!)

Ethics and the Buddha's Eight Fold Path.

If we look at the three areas under ethical conduct we can see the basis of living with integrity.

3: Right Speech

4: Right Action

5: Right Livelihood

Right Speech

The focus of the Right Speech is to avoid harmful language, such as lying or unkind words. It is far better to use gentle, friendly and meaningful words, even when a situation calls for a truth that may be hurtful, despite the follower's best intentions.

Right Action

The Right Action forms a list of fundamental ethical behaviours all practising Buddhists should follow. These are the <u>Five Precepts:</u>

1. To refrain from destroying living beings
2. To refrain from stealing
3. To refrain from sexual misconduct (adultery, rape, etc.)
4. To refrain from false speech (lying)
5. To refrain from intoxicants which lead to heedlessness.

Right Livelihood

Those seeking enlightenment should pick the Right Livelihood to support the other fundamentals of Buddhism. Followers should avoid employment in positions where their actions may cause harm to others, be it directly or indirectly.

Here we can see how the ethics in the eight fold path follow the ethics in the last five Commandments and also that these ethics have a base in system integrity – co-operation and contribution. *Right action, right speech, and right livelihood are the basis of integrity.*

I also find it interesting that the second commandment is similar to what the Buddha said. You shall not make for yourself a carved image - any likeness of anything that is in heaven above, or that is in the earth beneath, or that is in the water under the earth. How many images do you see in a Christian church or Buddhist temple? It makes them sectarian and I tend to think this was the reason why it was suggested that images should not be worshiped. It is the principles, not the image, which we need to embody. *The image is nothing more than imagination and can be distorted – the principles can be tested for truth.* A principle is a foundation upon which other values and measures of integrity are based.

If we live our lives through these principles, we meet our needs and the needs of others. We have integrity and the system maintains integrity. We continue to evolve. If we don't, we frustrate our needs and the needs of others. We fail to evolve. The universe doesn't discriminate. It appears to be an elegant system that seems to have a built-in safety mechanism that eliminates all who don't adapt to its changing conditions and evolve. Integrity follows the rules of cause and effect, chaos and stability.

Sociopathic tendencies may well be genetic but may also be learned - the ego's effort to protect the heart from pain and in so doing to harden it. Many criminals show remorse and learn lessons from a lack of integrity. They transform their lives into something better. A lack of integrity will always offer lessons to learn. If you don't learn the lesson you are doomed to repeat it.

There is a Prime Minister of Australia who promised before an election, never to bring in a carbon tax under the government she led. Without this promise she would never have been elected. Once in power she moved to bring in a carbon tax, a deal made with other parties and so called independent politicians seeking increased power. This lack of integrity created a massive slide in her approval. It had nothing to do with a carbon tax. Most people understand the need to reduce pollution. The rejection of her was all to do with the lie to gain power at all costs - the lack of integrity. Trust is a connecting habit. If we feel we can't trust someone we feel disconnected and disempowered. It is one of the reasons why politicians are the least trusted people in society. They far too often sacrifice honesty and integrity for power. I find it interesting that we don't usually say 'those in government,' we usually say 'those in power.' I also find it laughable that politicians call each other the *right honourable member* - nothing honourable in a lack of integrity.

We have integrity when we see ourselves as part of the whole

The word *integrity* stems from the Latin adjective *integer* (whole, complete). In the context of wholeness, integrity is the inner sense of *wholeness* deriving from qualities such as honesty and consistency of character. We have integrity when we see ourselves as part of the whole. We lack integrity when we are stuck in this limited and tiny *I, me and mine* of the ego - stuck in wanting and not giving. Respecting the individual rights of others to meet their needs is the first step to having integrity.

The old saying, 'Do unto others as you would have done to you' might be a good place to start.

Don't bother too much about the problems created by the egos of others. Karma would seem to be the basic universal law of cause and effect in action. It usually catches up on a person one way or another. They become victims of themselves. Accept that the system of integrity must win out at some time in the future and go with the flow - with an acceptance and an allowance of things. We can now see that with conscious choice comes responsibility; our ability to respond - to make a choice. What are you choosing? Are you choosing actions that have integrity or actions that lack integrity? This will determine how happy you are, whether you know it or not! Actions that come from a place of integrity may not give you what you want. They will give you what you need!

There are exceptions. If my wife asks if her bottom looks big in the dress she has tried on I will always say no. Why? If my wife likes her dress I don't want to spoil her happiness. Have I lost my integrity by saying this? If we look back to co-operation and contribution we can see that honesty is not a blunt instrument. It can be withdrawn if it hurts no one and causes no harm. The man told he has a serious illness may not tell the full truth to his family. It is designed to stop hurt rather than to deceive to cause hurt.

The purpose of a good business is to provide a service to the community and, in doing so, make a profit for its shareholders. Many businesses lose sight of this as top executives focus on maximising profits and their personal remuneration – not their service to the customer or the community in general.

The purpose of Government is to provide for the basic needs of the community – education, food, shelter, health and freedom from harm. It should provide basic resources and an environment where people can contribute and co-operate. Politicians are public servants. They should be serving the public not dictating to them.

Sociopaths have a high level of focus on their goals. Many make it to the top in their professions. They are focused , intense and never waver from their goal, but a foundation not tied to solid ground will falter.

PURPOSE, SOCIOPATHS, INTEGRITY AND ETHICS

The bushido code is a base of ethical and moral conduct and beliefs. The code has a base, contribution and co-operation, this is its purpose. The samurais integrity is based in this. To live without integrity is to live without courage and honour To live life from a code of ethics and conduct, is to live life with purpose and integrity.

We will always come across people, some sociopathic, that lack any ethical moral code of conduct or integrity. That's just life. It takes discipline to be virtuous and maintain your integrity.

CHAPTER 20

Understanding the Bully

The bully feels like a victim and tries to make a victim of others.

Here is an old rhyme from when I was a kid. 'Sticks and stones may break my bones but words can never hurt me.'

Why bother looking at the bully when it comes to sport or the bushido mindset? Because every athlete will come across bullying at some time in their career. People trying to intimidate and control them. From a coach to an opponent, you will see it everywhere.

Most verbal bullying comes in the form of disconnecting habits of communication. *This is external control psychology* as covered by William Glasser. They are, criticizing, complaining, threatening, blaming, nagging, punishing and bribing. The bullies feel disconnected and disempowered in their lives, and attack others to control them. In so doing, feel they have some sense of power. It's a knife that cuts both ways. It hurts the bully just as much as the one being bullied. This is the ego at its worst but, unlike the sociopath, the bully feels like a victim and tries to make a victim of others.

We take being bullied personally. It isn't personal. It's the bully's problem. They are the ones that feel powerless. If they didn't feel powerless they wouldn't need to bully others. If we don't take it personally we can't be bullied verbally. We should feel sorry for the bully. They don't live happy lives, poor things. Sociopaths are effective bullies. This comes from a hidden sense of rage that they have supressed and a lack of guilt or remorse.

The bully lives in fear, stuck in the mind. From the heart we can feel compassion for the poor souls and this frees us. There is another thing about bullies. They have usually been bullied in the past. It takes a bully to create a bully. They have low self-esteem and will usually target the weak to feel strong. The paradox is that they must feel weak to want to feel strong. Because of low self-esteem the ego wants to inflate itself to feel superior to others - again a paradox. You must feel inferior to others to want to feel superior to them and you must feel powerless to want power over others. Bullies often recruit others who feel weak to help them bully. This is often the choice; better to be on the side of the bully than to be bullied by them. Most bullies are cowards who live in fear.

Many parents bully their children without even knowing they are doing it. Many bosses bully staff at work thinking they are just doing their job. Once we realise that the disconnecting habits are our bullying behaviour, we can make amends. We have all been guilty of it at some time or other.

Many parents who were punished as children believe that, if it worked for them, it will work for their children. If we don't punish our children they won't learn what they are doing wrong. Punishment is a disconnecting habit. There is a simple tool I teach to clients to avoid using this disconnecting habit. I have the parents sit down with their children and come up with a set of rules they all agree on. The parents then negotiate the consequences of their children breaking these rules. Once a child accepts the negotiated consequence they are taking ownership of the consequence. If they break the rules it isn't the parent dishing out the punishment. They are punishing themselves. When the parent punishes a child, the child feels as though they are being bullied. If the child has agreed to the consequences of breaking the rules they must understand that they have a choice. Allowing a child to have a choice meets that child's need for empowerment. No one is trying to take their power away. If a child misbehaves, the parent just needs to point out the consequence that they have mutually chosen. The behaviour eventually stops because there is no battle between the parent's ego and the child's.

I find children will test the parent's resolve in following through with the consequences. The child has chosen the consequences so there is no need for the parent to feel guilty about following through with them. I find that this helps a child understand that there are consequences to all their actions. This is a good lesson to learn at an early age.

> **When we use disconnecting habits we are trying to control others.**

When we use disconnecting habits on others. It is bullying. As children we take it personally. As adults we can choose to take it personally. It isn't personal. It is the other person's problem so we don't need to take it personally. Some parents are still bullying their children long after they have grown into adults. Some parents still feel the need to control their children regardless of their age. They love their children but create problems in their relationship by trying to control them.

One of the best words you can use to yourself if someone is using disconnecting habits is – *Interesting*. Interesting places us in the position of the observer. If you find the bully's comments interesting, you are not taking them personally. Only the ego takes it personally. When I find a bully's comments interesting, it takes me to a place of wondering what their problem is.

Some bullies have passive-aggressive behaviour. These are the hard ones to pick. They tell you what you want to hear and then do something else. They can't say it to your face but work behind your back. To your face they never utter an unpleasant word, but, as they are walking out the door, their fiendish minds are working on a plot to bring you down or disrupt your plans, your suggestions or directions. Most passive-aggressive people feel insecure.

Passive-aggressive behaviour is a learned personality trait. Their passive, sometimes obstructionist resistance to following through with expectations in interpersonal or occupational situations can cause many problems. It is a personality trait marked by a pervasive pattern of negative attitudes and passive, usually disavowed, resistance in interpersonal or occupational situations. It can manifest itself as a learned helplessness, procrastination, stubbornness, resentment, sullenness, or deliberate and repeated failure to accomplish requested tasks. The passive-aggressive persons sees themselves as the victim of bullying – but they try to bully others by their actions. Passive-aggressive people often like to gossip. It is often a result of a problem with a parent in childhood or bullying, but it is a learned behavior and usually a sad sign of immaturity. Some passive-aggressive behaviours are designed to push your buttons to help to make them feel superior, but to avoid a reaction. One passive-aggressive person I know will often suggest, that people who think a certain way, or act a certain way are idiots. While knowing full well it's the way I would probably think or act. You know it's aimed at you but it is a comment designed to hurt and yet avoid conflict. I find it interesting that he needs to try to pull me and others, down through generalized judgmental comments to feel good. Like all bullies, he wants to feel superior, but must feel inferior to behave this way. I also find it sad because he is usually a very nice guy. It is designed to inflict pain, and yet avoid conflict. Once a passive-aggressive person decides not to like you, there is not much you can do to change it. They will tell you what you want to hear to your face, but you don't want to hear what they say behind your back. Their actions or lack of, are designed to frustrate you.

UNDERSTANDING THE BULLY

Most bullies are made - not born that way. They were created by circumstance. Cut them some slack and don't take it personally - It's their problem, not yours.

The Samurai were not bullies. Bullies are cowards that try to intimidate to control from a point of their own fear. The bully has no moral code of behaviour. A bully cant intimidate a person who operates from a moral and ethical code of conduct, they only feel threatened by them.

CHAPTER 21

Forgiveness

Forgiveness frees the forgiver as well as the forgiven

We have all been hurt by people in the past. Holding onto this hurt keeps us in the past and always a victim of the perpetrator. To forgive is not that easy and will often be rejected as not an option, but it is a choice. How can you forgive someone who abuses a child or rapes someone, or a person who kills another, or someone who steals from you and gets away with it?

These perpetrators and predators are the true losers in life. They could never be happy to commit these crimes in the first place and could never be happy after committing them. They are their own worst enemies. Stuck in the worst of their ego selves they create drama, and as a consequence that drama will be returned eventually. Sick and sad people are what they are, never to be happy. That's karma: They are victims of themselves. Forgiveness is about taking your power back.

Getting back the power that was taken from you. Why should you feel bad when you have done nothing wrong?

It takes courage to forgive - to let go of the hurt

You don't need to give the perpetrator a hug or talk to them to forgive. In most cases it would be best to avoid any contact with the perpetrator whatsoever. Some might have long since died or been imprisoned. They are all prisoners of their past actions and all losers because of these actions. I don't want to be the victim of a loser.

It takes courage to forgive - to let go of the hurt. The ego wants us to hold onto it. It thrives on being a victim. It only exists if we are victims. The biggest barrier to forgiving is the feeling of the injustice of it all. It isn't fair. However, bad things happen to good people. It is just a fact of life. Where egos abound there will be injustice. The more a person allows their ego to run the show, the more they will hurt others and be hurt. The ego of a person can always rationalise its reason for hurting others and the person will deny they are at fault. The person stuck in their ego hurts themselves as much as they hurt anyone else without even realising it. It's a knife that cuts both ways.

It is hard to forgive a bully without understanding their behaviour. Understanding that the bully must feel powerless, disconnected and disempowered to act the way they do can be the first step to dropping the injustice we feel.

Our reputation is in the hands of others. We have no control over it. Our character is in our own hands, no one can touch it. I have seen many good people have their reputations trashed by colleagues looking to further their own self-interests. Sometimes we need to forgive and forget. Sometime we need to forgive but not forget. Often we need to remember the type of person we are dealing with to protect ourselves from further harm. If we understand that the person doing the harm to us is doing it from their own place of suffering and creating more suffering for themselves. Then we can forgive from a point of compassion for the loser that they are, feel sorry for them, which is in turn a form of compassion. Sometimes we just need to say 'stuff them. They are just idiots and losers and I don't want to lose myself to them any longer. I am taking my power back.'

The greatest gift we can give ourselves is the gift of forgiveness. Only by choosing to forgive can we be truly free of the past and no longer victims of it.

CHAPTER 22

Ego States, Anchors and Triggers

> *Evoke the power of positive states - you have them too.*

We have looked at the ego as the accumulation of negative limiting beliefs. Let's look at this in a bit more detail. Let's say that each negative belief is a mini trauma from the past that was formed during a state of fear. The fear may have formed a feeling of helplessness or a feeling of not being worthy, of not being approved of. It could, for example, also be just insecurity that formed through loss or a feeling of not being safe or just being scared. It could have come from a time when we were bullied by someone, or maybe, as a young child, when we had just lost our parents in a supermarket. Or possibly a time when we felt abandoned, rejected or unable to live up to our parents' expectations. The possibilities are endless. The resultant beliefs are based on a fear of lack, a lack of approval, of control, of security.

At the time of this trauma, a state of fear would have presented itself, resulting in the flight or fight response - a basic physiological survival mechanism in response to a threat; a threat that could be physical or emotional in form. A belief is formed to protect us from future threats. In the event of a future threat, the belief will form a state of fear - an ego state similar to the initial event; a feeling of not being safe; or of being unworthy, just to name a few. These beliefs are limiting us from reaching our full potential, they keep us stuck.

We don't only have negative beliefs, we also have positive beliefs. These beliefs are usually built from an accumulation of positive things that happen to us: having loving supporting and encouraging parents; standing up for ourselves against a bully, or protecting a friend or younger sibling; and being treated with respect. It could come from our continuing achievements at school or in sport, or overcoming a perceived problem. The beliefs formed create feelings of confidence, empowerment, worthiness, approval and security. These beliefs are not limiting us; they grow as we build on them. They create positive states. When we feel threatened, the negatively threatened ego state will rise to the executive position and take control to protect us. It will take charge to become the dominant state. When this happens we sometimes no longer have access to the more positive states.

The negative ego states are anchored to an event. Similar events or situations will trigger an emotional fear response and this may result in a phobia of sorts. The things that can trigger this response are many and varied - often just imagined. A fear of public speaking has its roots in the past, as do phobias about snakes, flying or lifts, etc. The triggered ego state creates the anxiety - the fear of the future that dominates the imagination with this perceived threat. Logically the mind knows that there isn't anything to fear, but the subconscious is not rational or logical. The ego state refuses to listen to the logical mind; it takes control. In this state, other more positive states are ignored and protection is paramount. The traumatized ego state is running the show.

EGO STATES, ANCHORS AND TRIGGERS

The ego states are a function of the thought/feeling system but many negative ego states can be established from a response to a traumatic physical threat. My own feeling of claustrophobia when trying to snorkel for the first time is an example. My inability to take a breath with my head under water may well have come from breathing in water at bath time as a baby. This was overcome through desensitization by repeated practice with a snorkel - just as the phobia of speaking in public can be overcome through desensitization by practice.

I had a client who told me she would spontaneously vomit at the smell of a certain aftershave. She was gang raped at the age of fourteen and one of the rapists was wearing this aftershave when it happened. It was a subconscious reaction. I am continually amazed at how much pain we humans can inflict on each other. Especially emotional pain that can last a lifetime unless resolved. And most of the time, the perpetrator is probably unaware of the extent of the damage they actually create by their actions. It, in most cases, must be a result of the damage done to them at some time in the past.

Traumatic ego states often require therapy, to gain access to more positive states and allow the traumatized ego state to feel safe enough to allow positive states to play their part. Often we can gain access to the positive states through the use of anchors and triggers. It makes sense that if we can anchor and trigger negative ego states, then we can anchor and trigger positive ego states. The interesting thing is that athletes have been doing this for years, many without even knowing. The footballer who continues to wear the lucky underpants he was wearing when they won the championship two years earlier is doing so to trigger the anchor from that day. The routine of pulling up of both socks and then throwing a piece of grass in the air to test the wind before taking the kick is another example of triggering a state of mind - a positive state. Often in our work our negative ego states limit our ability to achieve all that we can. A fear of public speaking or cold calling clients is a good example. A negative ego state created through being rejected, not feeing approved of, or not feeling worthy, can create a barrier to achieving our full potential. Procrastination can be a result of this. We know what we need to do, but are afraid to do it. What if we get rejected? What if we are not approved of? What if we fail? We end up treading water and going nowhere, doing nothing. We need to step out of our comfort zone, and sometimes we need access to a positive state to do this. This is where anchors and triggers come in - to change our state.

A sales company sent one of their sales representatives to me for sales development. During one session we identified four potential new customers who could increase his sales and margins by 20 plus percent. He was given the task of setting up appointments with them. He returned two weeks later and made every excuse as to why he hadn't had the time to make contact. The negative ego state, fearing rejection, had created the procrastination. I had him imagine a time when he felt really confident, not concerned with failure or rejection. He thought about his time as a junior footy coach, a time when his football team was playing in a final. They hadn't expected to get that far, and he told the team it wasn't about winning but about playing the game to the best of their abilities. Regardless of the result he would be proud of them for trying. They won the game. I had him imagine giving this pep talk to his team and getting all the feelings associated with this event. I then had him clap his hands and rub the palms of his hands vigorously together so he could feel the heat from the friction between the palms, while saying in his mind, 'okay, let's just do it.' I told him to practice this over the next week. And anytime he felt he was putting things off, to clap his hands and rub the palms together while saying in his mind, 'okay, let's just do it.'

The purpose of this action is to anchor a positive resource - a positive state to a past positive experience. We can then trigger, through this anchor, the state of the positive experience when needed, to overcome the negative ego state. By the following appointment with me he had made contact and had appointments with the new potential customers.

EGO STATES, ANCHORS AND TRIGGERS

He had also found them quite accommodating and realised there had been nothing to fear but the fear itself.

> *The way we feel is always a result of the dominant ego state at the time*

This simple anchor and trigger technique can be very powerful. I use it in my work with athletes to get them focused or fired up, or for public speaking to create a strong expectation of a positive result. It can also be used for phobias, such as flying, to motivate and push past the fear, or overcome situational anxiety such as pre-exam nerves, or social anxiety. It is designed to trigger a positive expectation and overcome procrastination from a base of positive states. Change your state and you change your mind and the way you feel. - The way we feel is always a result of the dominant state at the time.

Anchors and triggers can be many and varied, and sometimes we don't realize we are triggering negative ego states. Our state is often reflected in our posture. A person feeling depressed will sit with head bowed and shoulders slumped. Just changing the posture by pulling shoulders back, head up or putting a smile on the face can change that state and the way we feel. Most followers of sport have seen the posture of a team that has already given in to defeat - they have dropped their heads, we might say. What they have actually done is to change their state to one resigned to defeat and failure, and this is reflected in their posture. It's hard to feel bad when you are smiling.

Let's cover the technique to anchor and trigger a positive state. First, we must access a positive experience from the past where we felt confident and motivated, or we can create this from an imagined future experience. For example, in public speaking we can imagine giving the presentation, being dynamic and giving it with confidence and passion. We are creating all the feelings we would feel hearing the applause and kind words afterwards.

Once the state of confidence, calmness, excitement, achievement, etc. is achieved, it needs to be anchored. I believe the best anchor comprises of two elements, an action and a feeling; such as clapping the hands together and rubbing the palms to generate heat. I have also used rubbing the thumb and forefinger together. It can also be as simple as straightening the strings on a tennis racket between shots, or bouncing a basketball three times and saying focus each time to create a focused concentration. Imagine or remember a positive experience, and get in touch with the positive feelings you would feel from this happening; then anchor. The more it is practised the stronger the anchor to the feeling and positive state. We are anchoring the good feelings.

I can't help but be excited and motivated to action by just rubbing my hands together. This trigger gets me excited. I use it prior to giving workshops and seminars. It is also useful when I need to get motivated to do an account reconciliation or quarterly tax statement - not amongst my favorite chores!

Our vocabulary also triggers ego states

I have long since dropped the words 'angry' and 'frustrated' from my vocabulary and replaced them with 'perturbed' and 'interesting'. I have no ego state that can latch onto the word 'perturbed'. In fact the word makes me laugh to myself. I have never developed an ego state association with the word *perturbed* the way I have developed an association with the word *angry*. If I say to myself that I am angry, an angry ego state pops up. If I say I am frustrated, a frustrated ego state pops up. If I say that's interesting, I become the observer of the situation and not a frustrated participant. Hate is another triggered ego state that is often used with such abandon - from food to traffic jams or people or professions or even work. 'I hate being stuck in traffic', you might say, without realising how it will make you feel. It can't help but make you feel bad, and yet it isn't good or bad; it just is. Why feel bad about something you have no control over? The negative words you use to describe your situation will trigger a negative ego state and the associated feelings.

I often tell a client who presents with depression to remove the word 'depression' from their vocabulary. It represents a long dark tunnel with no end in sight. I tell them to say they are down, and they can pick themselves up; or sad, and they can do something to make themselves happy. With anxiety I will tell them to say they are just scared, and ask themselves 'what am I scared of?' A lot of the time they are just scared of being anxious! A fear of fear.

Our negative words are often anchors from the past that will trigger the negative ego state. Remove the negative words from your thoughts and conversation and you can't help but feel better. Use positive self-talk especially when talking about yourself, or your life situation to yourself or to others and improve the way you feel.

Let your posture reflect the way you want to feel - confident, relaxed, alert and happy. If you are happy, you will infect others with your happiness. Let your words be positive, not negative, and learn to trigger positive states then notice the difference in the way you feel.

MINDSET OF THE WARRIOR

CHAPTER 23

Comfort Zones

> *Your comfort zone is either expanding or contracting*

Comfort zones, what are they?

We are always in a state of expansion or contraction, growing or shrinking, progressing or regressing. Let's take our muscles, or even better, the muscles of a football player, or athlete, for example. After a period of rest and reduced activity, at the end of a season, the muscles have begun to lose strength and shrink before the training for the new season begins.

Those first few training sessions result in stiffness and soreness as the muscles get pushed beyond what has become comfortable use in the off season. They start to feel discomfort. The athlete must push beyond what feels comfortable to grow in strength, fitness and endurance and this will continue throughout the season. Every time they push past what is comfortable and break through that comfort zone they are growing. If they don't push past that comfort zone they are stagnating or regressing.

This push past the comfort zone must be done gradually to avoid injury. This is true for athletes and also true for our emotional comfort zone that is the limit of the positive beliefs we have about ourselves - the limit of our positive self-esteem.

> ***To grow we must do things that make us feel uncomfortable***

Outside our comfort zone are the negative limiting beliefs about ourselves; the ego. The ego is always telling us we are not good enough, not accepted, not approved of and not worthy. Many of these beliefs were formed when we were children - when people used disconnecting habits on us, or withdrew connecting habits - beliefs formed before we had a rational faculty of mind. Imagine a ball full of positive energy, positive beliefs, sitting in the centre of a field of negative energy and negative beliefs. The field of negative beliefs places pressure and stress on the ball of positive beliefs and the positive beliefs are pushing back - the ball expanding and contracting. For the ball to expand, we must push past negative beliefs that make us feel uncomfortable. To grow we must do things that make us feel uncomfortable. The negative beliefs form a barrier we must push through.

Let's take a look at public speaking, said to be the number one fear of many people. Why is it a fear? It's the want for approval. The fear that people won't accept the way we look, what we have to say or how we are saying it. If we take a logical look at this fear, we can see it is an irrational fear and without justification; impossible to satisfy. It is impossible to get the approval of everyone. In fact it is almost impossible to get one person's approval all the time. If I could get my wife's approval all the time it would be fantastic, but in reality it won't happen, I am not perfect. If you had 51% of people's approval, you could become prime minister of the country. This limiting fear, the fear that we will not be approved of, is the discomfort we feel pushing back on our comfort zone, making us feel uncomfortable. Our comfort zone is the limit of our positive beliefs.

The amazing thing about expanding your comfort zone is that, when you tackle one limiting belief, many other similar ones fall away; you grow exponentially and increase your self-esteem. When we are growing, our self-esteem is high and when we are shrinking, our self-esteem is low. When it comes to public speaking, every time you push past the fear it becomes easier. But, like anything, it must be done gradually. In my experience, it can take 4 to 6 weeks to change the habit patterns of the mind.

I had a friend who had no problem with public speaking. He said he loved it and asked me what the difference was between him and so many others that seemed so terrified. I told him that he expected everyone would like him and didn't bother about wanting their approval. He agreed that he did expect everyone to like him. I looked at him and said, 'Not everyone is going to like you.'

'That's their problem not mine' was his reply.

Apart from comfort zones formed by the way we have been treated in life; we can also develop a fear from a trauma that can become a phobia, or a problem with anxiety or depression. If our comfort zone is limited by a phobia, sometimes the cause of this phobia isn't self-apparent. Let me tell you about a phobia I discovered in myself in my late twenties.

The first time I went snorkelling was in my twenties. Friends gave me a mask and snorkel and we waded off into the sea. I was looking forward to seeing this new underwater world. I put my face into the water and could not for the life of me take a breath through the snorkel. I was crippled by fear - something was telling me I couldn't breathe with my face underwater. Lifting my head from the water and looking around at my friends all snorkelling away, I tried again but the breath wouldn't come. My ego being what it was at that time, I watched my friends snorkel and as each one popped his head up I held my breath, put my head down and pretended to snorkel. When we returned to the beach I told them how much I'd enjoyed it and was off to buy a mask and snorkel for myself. Over the next month I would get into the bath each night and practise. One or two breaths on the first session, but increasing as the days went on until I could spend a full hour with my head submerged, breathing through a snorkel. Not one to do things by halves, my next trip to the beach was to scuba dive. I convinced a friend who scuba dived to take me out and teach me to dive. We jumped out of his boat with a compressor running in the background feeding air to the regulators in our mouths. Thirty feet below us was the sea bed. I was bobbing like a cork on the surface when he suggested that I might not have enough lead weight around my waist. I didn't like the idea of carrying this lead anchor around my waist, but I was told it was required to compensate for the buoyancy of the very uncomfortable and very thick wet suit he had arranged for me to wear. I told him I thought the current weight would be fine. Breathing out, he started to descend. Breathing out, I was still bobbing on the surface like a cork. Eventually he was on the bottom when I decided to duck dive down and, thrashing like a fish out of water I made it to the bottom. The first thing I noticed was the excruciating pain in my ears, and the second thing I noticed was my feet were still pointing to the surface. Upside down, I grappled with the weeds on the sea bed to try to keep myself on the bottom. He gave the thumbs up signal rehearsed in the boat. With both hands busy, I smiled and the water filled the mask. Like an unguided missile, I launched out of the water breeching like a hump - backed whale.

We returned to the boat and removed my mask to find it filled with watery blood. 'Didn't you equalise?' my friend asked.

'What's that?' I asked. The vacuum from the water pressure had sucked blood into my sinuses, I found out later.

> **We extend our comfort zones by releasing the negative emotion attached to the fear**

'Maybe we should give it a miss', he said. I knew, at that point, that giving it a miss would mean I would not be coming back. We adjusted the weight. I learned how to equalise the pressure and I dived for the next thirty minutes without pain or a problem. Within three years I was a scuba diving instructor. Within five years I was teaching instructors and diving in the limestone caves of South Australia, my comfort zone well and truly extended. This extension of my comfort zone had been through desensitisation. Each small step outside the comfort zone tackled the limiting belief and I was growing exponentially. Had I not tackled this limiting belief, I would have missed out on a whole range of wonderful experiences, and a whole group of new friends in the process. We extend our comfort zones by releasing the negative emotion attached to the fear.

We can overcome limiting beliefs and extend our comfort zones regardless of the cause of these limiting beliefs. By extending our comfort zones we increase our self-esteem and grow as people. The limiting beliefs are not you; they are irrational fears designed to protect you. But in the end they only limit you. They are just an electro chemical process in the body, created by an electro chemical process in the brain, created by negative conditioning from the past. They are a distorted view of who you are - an illusion of who you are.

The workplace is often a place where people work within their comfort zones unless a positive environment and culture is created to change this. If a boss manager uses disconnecting habits on employees, they will be afraid to fail, and this closes down creativity. They will be afraid they won't be approved of. The comfort zone of a person under a boss manager will contract and shrink as the disconnecting habits tap into limiting negative beliefs.

With a lead manager we will experience the opposite - the employee's comfort zones will expand and grow as the connecting habits are used on them. They will become more creative and push to achieve greater goals with positive expectations. They can step out of their comfort zones with support and encouragement. They will enjoy an environment and a culture of challenge, support and encouragement.

We can see the same situation arising with a coach or trainer. It is important for an athlete to have a coach or trainer that continually challenges an athlete's comfort zone in a positive way. Both physically and mentally.

To grow as a person we need to take on challenges that make us feel uncomfortable. When we look at goal setting we will see that the goals should be big enough to scare us a little and excite us a lot.

When you start to step outside your comfort zone you begin to realise that there is nothing to fear but the fear itself. So go out now and do something that challenges you; do something that makes you feel uncomfortable. Push yourself beyond your comfort zone, increase your self-esteem and grow into your true self.

From the point of view of the 'Warrior Mindset', an ethical, morale code of conduct is the foundation from which to expand your comfort zone. Self-control and discipline will create the expansion of skillset and mindset.

CHAPTER 24

Goal Setting and Time Management

> *Everything we do comes from a goal set in the subconscious mind*

Purpose and Motivation and Goals

Your goal is the purpose for what you do. Without a clearly defined goal you will lack the purpose to achieve it. Everything you do should be with this purpose in mind, to achieve your goal. Your goal can have many reasons. Your purpose has only one, achieving your goal. The purpose of achieving your goal creates the motivation to achieve it. Purpose and motivation are entwined. A goal is just a dream; with purpose it creates motivation to bring it to reality.

Walt Disney once said that all dreams come true if you have the courage to pursue them.
I always introduce clients to goal setting; it creates a positive expectation of the future – something many people don't have. Goals

motivate, excite and create momentum.

How many dreams have you squandered in your life through lack of action and commitment? We have all had dreams, but often we lose sight of them as the trivialities of day to day existence take us away from pursuing them. These are trivialities for which we often sacrifice our important dreams. These short-term wants take us away from our long-term aspirations – away from our goals and our dreams. What we will be covering in this chapter are the simple steps of goal setting and time management.

I had a client who worked for IBM. I suggested we look at goal setting and, he told me he had recently done a five day course on goal setting so it was probably pointless. I asked what goals he had been working on since the course and he said he hadn't developed any yet. I think it might have been a case of too much information. You need to keep things simple for them to be effective and I would be at a loss to cover effective goal setting in more than one hour. I like to keep things simple.

Everything we do is goal orientated; it's the way the mind works and most goals are designed to meet our needs in some way. Just getting up to make a cup of coffee starts as a goal in the mind. With goal setting, we are looking at setting goals that help us grow. Because of this a goal should be big enough to scare us a little but also excite us a lot. Sometimes it is fear that stops us achieving our goals. Fear of failure can stop us dead in our tracks. Sometimes we just feel overwhelmed by the things we need to do to reach the goal, or the time it will take to reach it. Sometimes we feel that we just don't have enough time. Well you can't eat an elephant in a single sitting but you can eat it one bite at a time. Some simple steps can overcome these barriers.

Around 3% of people write down their goals – only 3%. But it has long been recognised that the 3% are the ones most likely to reach their goals.

GOAL SETTING AND TIME MANAGEMENT

> *Working on three to five goals on a continuing basis allows us to achieve the things we would like on a regular basis*

Let's first look at goals from a business point of view. How far do you think we would get if we said let's build a 20 story building over there and not write anything down? How far would we get if we didn't turn it into a project and plan the activities from design to construction? It might seem ridiculous but that's exactly what most people do when it comes to their own goals. Your own goals and dreams need to be turned into personal projects – some large projects and some small projects. When you can see your goals as projects, you can plan the activities to accomplish them; you can move them from wishful thinking to reality. I believe that working on three to five goals on a continuing basis allows us to achieve the things we would like on a regular basis.

Let's again look at the project of building a 20 story building. The goal first must start in the imagination of someone. If you look around and see all the man-made things your eyes come to rest upon, you can understand that they all started out in someone's imagination – chairs, computers, cars, cups, clothes and that's just to name a few! They all started out as someone's dream. All started out as an imagination that moved to a business project that materialised through planning and activity. In business we can be quite good at allocating time and resources to the bigger projects and yet still not see most of our work time as *working on a project* time. There should be times for maintenance that can also be a project. If we are not working on projects of growth, then there is a good chance we are stagnating or going backwards.

What is time? Can we actually make time, lose time or buy time? Not really. Time is just a period of measurement. As the earth rotates on its axis, it gives us periods of days, and as it orbits the sun gives us periods of years. All periods of time for humans are psychological time – we created them. We break the days into hours, and the hours into minutes – but it is all created in the minds of people. Some organisms have their own sense of time, such as the corals on the great-barrier reef. They spawn once a year over a two day period – but this is a result of environmental conditions. They don't follow the human clock. (And they chose to spawn a few days after I spent a week in Queensland waiting to see this marvellous thing happen!)

You can't manage time; but we can plan time to manage activities. It is a psychological resource – a resource given in the same amount to everyone every day. It's the activities you choose to perform and the management of these activities within a set time frame that determines whether goals are being achieved. So we can't make time, but we can take the time we have in this moment to do what's important. We can take the time to plan and perform activities each day that will move us closer towards our goals.

So, let's look at the mechanics of goal setting. I believe it was Napoleon Hill in his book *Think and grow rich*, who first said, 'what you can conceive and believe; you can achieve.'

So, the goal or dream starts in the imagination as a concept. We start to visualise the finished result. Because the subconscious mind can't tell the difference between a real or imagined experience, the more we hold the goal in our imagination the more real it becomes for us. It becomes believable – and when it is believable the subconscious mind moves us towards it, what we believe we will see. Maxwell Maltz wrote a best-selling book called *'Psycho-Cybernetics'* back in the seventies – psycho being the mind and cybernetics being a guidance system much like we see in a plane or a guided missile. A plane or guided missile may be off target over 95% of the time but it keeps checking progress towards the target and altering direction to suit. When we imagine our goal as realised on an ongoing basis the subconscious mind works the same way. It becomes creative in checking progress and changing direction, if required, to get back on track.

GOAL SETTING AND TIME MANAGEMENT

> *We need to turn the want into an expectation and know we will achieve it*

To make sure we hold the goal in our imagination we need to write it down with a time frame and visualise it frequently. When writing down a goal, always write the goal with a time frame and as though it is already realised – this creates a positive expectation. We don't want to hold it in our mind as a want. This will just tap into the fear that we may not get what we want. We need to turn the want into an expectation and know we will achieve it. I have a ring binder exercise pad to write down my goals.

I worked with another Psychotherapist as his supervisor. When he first came I mentioned the benefit of giving clients CDs for use between sessions and suggested he would benefit from doing the same. Each month he would come along for supervision and I would ask how his CD was coming along, only to get the same answer: 'I've started the script but haven't had the time to work on it.'

The following is the way I turned the idea of the CDs into reality. This comes directly from my goal book and it is this simple.

The Goal.
By the end of November I have three new tracks to add to the car CDs.

To Do.
Track name
Ego states   ~~Write script~~   Record
Attitude   ~~Write script~~   Record
Moment   ~~Write script~~   Record

A script for a 15 to 20 minute recording will take me around four hours to write. I will record the three tracks together and allow eight hours for recording, editing and adding music. Total time is twenty hours. I take the ego states script and book two 1 hour sessions in my diary each week for the next two weeks. I scribe a line through this to let me know it is in the diary. At the end of the two weeks this is now complete and is highlighted with a yellow highlighter. The next script is then allocated time in the diary and a line scribed through it. The above example tells me I have two scripts finished and one in progress and I am now looking at booking in the eight hours for recording.

The more yellow I see, the more motivated I become to achieve the end results. This goal was achieved over a seven week period. I write 'completed' through the goal when finished and leave a few of these completed goals in the front of my goal book. This tells me each time I open my goal book how good I am at achieving them – simple, but very effective.

It is the same principle for personal or business goals. Holding the goal in the imagination is the first step to achieving it, but our management activities make the difference between achieving a goal and letting it drop off the radar.

Now this is where we need to look at a goal in the same way as a business looks at a large project: with a list of things to do; plus a list of activities that needs to be completed for the goal to be realised. So we put together a 'to do' list with all the activities needed to achieve the goal. I always suggest that you have an exercise book where you write down your goals and list the activities to do.

This might be a 'to do' list for the person wanting to get fit and lose 5 kg.

- Forty-five minutes of exercise 5 times a week.
- Limiting eating treats to twice a week. Small treat.
- Eating healthy food for all meals. Higher protein lower carbs.
- Two meals open choice. No restrictions on type of food.
- Five alcohol free days a week.

Now we know what to do, we need to schedule when to do it in a diary. Schedule the exercise on five days at the times you plan to do it. Nominate two days when treats are allowed and two open choice meals. Decide when you will have the alcohol-free days and nominate them with an 'AFD' in the diary. As this is a repeating schedule it can be duplicated each week in the diary, and in this case the project would run until the end of the year. At that time, you might consider retaining some of the key elements, such as exercise, as a maintenance program. The main thing to recognise is that you must keep the appointments with yourself. You must do what you have recognised you need to do to reach your goal or you will be drifting around the ocean like a ship without a rudder. Once you have scheduled your actions and given them a time-frame during your day, your goal is already realised. You just need to keep these appointments with yourself, but you have to be careful. In will pop the short term wants, 'I can't be bothered exercising today, I just want to stay in bed an extra half hour.' To overcome these wants we need to maintain the desire and motivation to reach the goal. We need to create a belief in its success – a positive expectation of a successful outcome. We need to develop the habit of doing what we need to do.

Your subconscious mind can't tell the difference between a real or imagined experience

In the case of this goal, each day you could visualise yourself as being fit and healthy and 5kg lighter, and feel the way you would feel if you were. Feel the way you would feel if it were already realised. It is our imagination, coupled with emotion, which creates the belief. Your subconscious mind can't tell the difference between a real or imagined experience. You might go through your goals each day and check progress towards them or you may find it suits you to do it once per week when you schedule the activities from your 'to do' list, but you should have your goals in your imagination at least once per day to maintain momentum and expected progress towards them.

There is another benefit from scheduling your day in a diary. It frees your mind to live in the moment – to be fully focused on the task at hand and this in turn makes you more efficient. Our minds no longer jump back and forth thinking I have to do this and that – it's all planned and in the diary or on the 'to do' list. And we can also have a daily 'to do' list for all those things that crop up from time to time that are not part of our goals.

Sometimes we can begin to feel overwhelmed by all the things we need to do. Listing and scheduling them takes our minds off them. We don't need to think about them until we do them. One of the most important things to schedule into your diary is a time each week to review your goals.

So let's review the basics of goal setting and time or activity management.

Firstly, see your goals as personal projects. Write them down with a time frame, and state them as though they are already realised. Have a goal book that you review at least once a week.

Secondly, break the goal down to activities you need to do to reach the goal.

Thirdly, schedule the activities into a diary and keep these appointments with yourself. Scribe a line through the activity in your goal book when you scheduled it in your diary. Highlight the activity in yellow in the goal book when it finished.

Do what you need to do. Keep these appointments with yourself and just do what you need to do in the moment.

Lastly, visualise them every day as you move towards them. As you do the activities and review them at least once a week, highlight the activities finished and schedule the next activity in your diary.

I see goals as organic and not set in stone. Sometimes goals will change or develop into something else. Let them grow and change if they need to.

CHAPTER 25

Unharnessed Aggression

Aggression:- definition

Aggression, in its broadest sense, is behaviour, or a disposition, that is forceful, hostile or attacking. It may occur either in retaliation or without provocation.

Aggressive energy has a valid place in the fight or training if it is harnessed and unleashed in a forceful and attacking way at the right time. It then becomes assertive.

Aggression plays a great part in many sports. Aggression in its simplest meaning is: any offensive action, attack or procedure. In psychiatry: it is overt or suppressed hostility, either innate or resulting from continued frustration and directed outward or against oneself.

In any sport it would be impossible to win without any offensive action or attack, so aggression in sport is not bad thing, it is just a valuable and necessary part of sport. Where it creates problems for the mindset of the athlete; is when it comes from a subconscious suppressed frustration or hostility. The problem is: If it is suppressed in the subconscious, we are often not aware of it until it explodes to life often at the wrong time, and when the genie is out of the bottle, it is hard to get it back in again. Often aggression takes on the cloak of impatience and frustration that we direct towards ourselves and others.

Your train your body in skill sets. The program for these skill sets reside in the subconscious like a computer program. The subconscious mind is a perfect servant. These programs become habitual behaviour without conscious thought. You train your mind to drive a car, it is difficult at first; you have to think about it. After a while the subconscious takes over and you are driving down the road thinking of something else, while the subconscious steers the car and keeps you at the right speed. Should something happen on the road ahead, the subconscious will soon hand the situation back to the conscious mind to make some choices. The subconscious doesn't make decisions and has no choices. It is the conscious mind that has choice and one choice we have is what to focus on.

An example in sport might be Jack Nicholas. He once said he expected to make 7 bad shots in a round. (His bad shots would be most people's good shots). If he played a bad shot he just accepted this was one of them and dropped any focus on it. It didn't disturb his mind and had no effect of his next shot. How many golfers carry one bad shot onto the next by getting angry about the last shot? The last shot is gone, you can't get it back; it's in the past. How many athletes take a loss or frustrations into the next event?

To understand unharnessed aggression we need to understand that it comes from a point of fear. The samurai understood it, but do our modern day warriors? The unbalanced mind is a mindset filled with fear. Fear is the greatest enemy of the warrior mindset: Irrational, illogical

UNHARNESSED AGGRESSION

fear. There is no doubt that in life that we will come across some rational fears, but it is the irrational and illogical fears that create most of the problems that create a disturbance in the mind. It is the subconscious mind that is the powerhouse of our abilities; the conscious mind is the tool to focus these abilities.

We are sure that many will be wondering how the unharnessed rage of one man can be turned on another with devastating results, and can come from a point of fear. Have no doubt that you will come to this understanding as you work through this book. You will be also given techniques to let go of any irrational and illogical fears that may be holding you back; but more of that later.

Although we might be looking at the ancient samurai for our first understanding of the warrior mindset, everything is being tested against modern psychological principals, from William Glasser's 'Choice Theory' to Viktor Frankle's' Existentialism' and cognitive behavioral therapy.

We will look at the processing power of the subconscious mind compared to conscious mind in the next chapter. We will then look at the understanding of the irrational illogical fears that hinder the warrior mindset.

The negative thoughts and unharnessed aggression result in one thing. Negative results.

From the samurai mindset, unharnessed aggression is a lack of self-control and often a lack of respect for others. It is power without focus and direction. It unbalances the mind. There is no doubt about its implication in the mindset of and athlete. From golfers to fighters, unharnessed aggression interrupts the natural flow of information from the subconscious mind to the body and this is where the problems stem from for many athletes.

CHAPTER 26

Attitude

Attitude

An attitude can be defined as a positive or negative evaluation of people, objects, event, activities, ideas, or just about anything in your environment.

Any negative evaluation will create a negative attitude. We are only interested in creating a positive attitude. Holding on to the past can create a negative attitude.

Highlighted: Quotes by Lou Holtz.

Past successful coach, Notre Dame, American football Team.

Ability is what you're capable of doing. Motivation determines what you do. Attitude determines how well you do it.

A positive attitude to hard work in training develops the habit of a good work ethic. The habit of doing the hard yards in training develops a positive attitude and confidence coming into a competition. **No one has ever drowned in sweat.** To be the best you must work harder than the rest.

I think everyone should experience defeat at least once during their career. You learn a lot from it.

The attitude we can develop from evaluating a loss can be positive if we are willing to learn the lessons from it. Learn, adjust and drop it.

You're never as good as everyone tells you when you win, and you're never as bad as they say when you lose.

What people say to us or about us are their opinions, not necessarily the truth. You can choose to accept them or reject them. We need to develop the attitude of not buying into them and taking them personal, they are just an opinion from someone else's ego viewpoint.

You'll never get ahead of anyone as long as you try to get even with him.

A grudge is a negative attitude towards someone. The ego is saying, "You have hurt me and now I want to hurt you". **Do right. Do your best. Treat others as you want to be treated.** The ego wants us to be a victim, it was how it was created and how it feeds and reinforces itself.

Lou Holtz didn't like his players showing elation after a win or deflation after a loss. It was just business, win or lose. Many coaches are good at strategy and skill training but understand nothing about mindset and their impact on it. The coach of football club asked me to give a talk about sport psychology to his team who had won the Victorian Southern League Grand Final the year before, but lost their first five games of the current season. I had concluded that they had become complacent in training due to over confidence. (Inflated ego and lack of purpose)

I met with him prior to discuss the presentation and to make sure there was no conflict in what I was about to say and what he was doing. At the end of my presentation to him he looked at me and said. "I have just realized that I am a big part of the problem". He had used disconnecting habits after the first loss, scathing in his criticism on the team and individuals, this had gotten worse as the losses mounted. He was a good tactical and skill training coach but didn't realize the negative impact his words were having on mindset of the players.

CHAPTER 27

Work Ethic and Training

> Work ethic and training comes from motivation. Motivation comes from belief. What you believe you can achieve.

If you don't believe it you can't achieve it and you won't be motivated to try. I am a great believer in only focusing on goals you can achieve. At 67 years old it is pointless aiming for athletic goals beyond my capabilities. My poor old body has neither the strength or endurance to compete with the younger bodies out there. There are many athletes that perform well into their mid-forties.

Work ethic and training will give you so much but genetics and life can take it away. 45 years old is probably a barrier to achieving great things in sport because of the declining ability of the body. That doesn't mean to say you can't achieve great things in older age. Cliff Young was a ultra-marathon runner from Australia. A potato farmer that just wouldn't stop running. He achieved at the age of sixty what people thought was impossible. Cliff wasn't physically gifted, just determined. He ran when everyone else rested. Endurance and mindset won him the race. He saw possibilities where other saw probabilities. I don't have Cliffs tenacity nor his goals. Cliff practiced by running for hours each day on his farm. Cliff was not a professional runner. Cliff was unheard of until the day he won the Melbourne to Sydney run against professional runners from all over the world. Cliff was a simple man that decided to run, and run he did. Day in and day out he ran and broke the record for an endurance race.

We can see people who are not the norm. Work ethic and training is their advantage. Cliff's slow shuffle was not what most would consider running, but running it was. Cliff's belief that he needed less time to recover and sleep than everyone else made the difference. Cliffs work ethic and training made the difference.

Who knows what set Cliff out on this quest, boredom or the opportunity to be more? All that is certain is his work ethic and training cemented his place in the world as a world class ultra-marathon runner. Age can be a barrier in some sports but not in all sports.

When it comes to work ethic and training, basically it comes down to goal setting. If you organise your time around your goal and do what you need to do to achieve your goal during this time, you have work ethic.

Simple and common sense but common sense is not that common.

Doing what you need to do.

There are always a number of things we would rather be doing than what we need to do and this is the problem. We focus on short term wants and not out long term needs.

Work ethic, is a habit of doing what you need to be doing to the best of your ability there and then. There are times we do it, but not to the best of our abilities; We slide by. Not the stuff that champions are made of.

WORK ETHIC AND TRAINING

Work ethic is doing your best every time you train or compete. It becomes a habit; second nature.

Without sight of a worthy goal the motivation to work is less. Why would you punish yourself for nothing? To excel you need to push through your comfort zone; push through what is comfortable. This is uncomfortable but you don't grow by staying comfortable.

OK. It is painful to grow; to be better than you are. Of course it is! That's why there is so few people reach the top. You have to go through a lot of pain, and we don't like pain. We seek pleasure. Embracing pain to reach a long term goal is what makes us so different to other animals. Through chaos we achieve evolution and adapt. The body has brilliant means of adaptation. The body will build what it doesn't possess.

This is why a body builder can build a body that is so alien to the normal person. If we push the body to an extreme it will build more potential based on its lack. There is as we can see at the moment, no limit to this, records keep getting broken. The body will build potential were it is lacking in potential.

Six sprints until you are out of breath over a period of 20 minutes, 3 times per week, will not only change the body's metabolism for 48 hours, but will also build the heart and lung capacity. It balances the body's sugar levels and builds cardio-pulmonary capacity. It works out at around 3 minutes per day, every second day. A reduction in the potential for diabetes and heart problems in the test subjects.

This is one of the reasons why Olympic records continue to be broken. What is the limit to this potential. Some may say physical but I would say mental. The four minute mile barrier was a good example. As soon as it was broken everyone was breaking it.

How can a 60 year old farmer and ultra-marathon runner, Cliff Young, beat professional runners if not for belief. How can we continue to beat every Olympic record if not for belief. Genetics has its hand in this but the mind is all powerful.

Work ethic, like everything else we are good at, comes from habit. We habitually act a certain way or think a certain way. Belief and goals power the focus, but habits are learned through repetition.

To have good work ethic we need to focus with a strong belief on achieving our goals. This creates the motivation to excel and push harder. We need to allocate time to achieve the goal. We need to make sure we push ourselves at these opportunities. We need to get into the habit of never missing these opportunities. We need to get into the habit of thinking and acting with full conviction.

CHAPTER 28

Work and Life Balance

> *I think the biggest problems for most athletes is work and life balance.*

It is hard to focus on your sport if your personal life is going down the tube. A problem for many athletes. You can get so focused on your athletic goals your personal life takes a second seat.

Your athletic goal is secondary to your primary goal. To by happy. If you allow your secondary goal to be all important your primary goal will be frustrated. If you are a happy person all other goals are a compliment to this primary goal.

Again we come back to the Bushido code. The primary goal is to be happy based on a life of ethics and morality.

What is the point of being a world champion if you are not happy?

A successful life is a happy life; everything else is just icing on the cake.

So many athletes get caught up in the celebrity status and the ego inflating itself. The next generation will forget you. You are a fleeting ideal in this generation. You are not perfect; you know it as well as I do.

People like to think of themselves better than others. The domain of the ego. All are created equal. No one is better than others. The ego wants to inflate its superiority because it feels inferior. You are not inferior or superior, but the ego wants to make it so. To feel superior to some must make you feel inferior to others. What a terrible way to feel.

In an athletic situation this type of superior/ inferior situation can get much worse based on past results. This of course would result in this negative mindset that will undermine performance.

If you employ what has been pointed out in the previous chapters on connecting habits and disconnecting habits. I am sure you will see an improvement. But you really need to dedicate time to building and maintain relationships. You need to make time for the people that love you and the people you love.

To be happy we need balance in our life. To find balance we need to spread our time and focus on other things. As a professional athlete your sport is your job, but it can't be the only thing in your life. You need to allocate time to spend with friends and family. Have other interests or hobbies. We need to work to live, but so many people live to work. On your death bed do you really think you will be looking back wishing you had spent more time in the gym or at work. I don't think so. Most people will look back on their life and wish they had spent more time with the people they love.

Relationships can break down when one person is more committed to the job than the relationship. To find balance we must allow time for all aspects of our lives. I get a lot of clients who don't have good memories of a parent. Some say they were never there for them, they were too focused on their work to spend time with their family. These children grow up into adults who feel they were not important and often not loved. This can create problems for them in adult life. Not having that balance between work and family can create family problems down the track.

When we get into the habit of total focus on work it becomes harder to switch off and enjoy yourself.

> **Allocating time for other people and interests is necessary to create balance in your life.**

At the end of a career so many athletes find themselves lost. Their identity was tied to their sport and what they achieved, or didn't achieve. Many lack a new direction and don't know what to do. The ego is often tied to the identity of being a professional athlete. Many athletes go off the rails at the end of their career. We see the same identity crisis in mothers when their children leave home. Their identity was all about being a mother and when the children leave home they lose their identity and get depressed. It is called empty nest syndrome. It also happens to some men when they retire from work or are unable to work. Their identity is tied to being a provider. Depression can kick in, some die before their time and some isolate themselves from their families feeling useless. I have the label of a psychotherapist. Psychotherapy is just something I do, not who I am. I have many roles, father, grandfather, husband, friend and the list goes on. If the ego attaches its identity to one role, it often neglects all others.

There must be some goals for the future to avoid this problem. It may be a move in a different direction. Some find jobs in coaching or television. The athlete who has life balance will not find it so hard to transition into new employment or fields.

> **It is hard to transition into another fields if you have been totally focused on the one thing.**

There are a few areas to look at.

Family - Find time to spend with them.

Friends- Cut loose and enjoy yourself.

Do something for your community.

Have some other personal goals and hobby's to focus on.

CHAPTER 29

Culture and Morale

Co-operation and contribution can overcome cultural differences

Cultural differences are the result of our conditioning. The culture of a people is a direct result of the conditioning based on the people around them. Many cultural differences come from different belief systems formed by this conditioning. Interaction between different cultures results in an expansion of both. Often the opposite is also true. What should be assimilation often turns to alienation because of our conflicting beliefs. Most conflict comes from rigid religious or racial beliefs.

What is normal? Nothing! What seems normal to one person seems abnormal to another. It is difficult to understand others from our own limited cultural belief system. No two people have the same life experiences or are exposed to the same cultural beliefs. There can be similarities based on similar beliefs. But different personalities and life experiences will create different belief systems. No two people can see the world in the identical way. We are all looking at the world through a different set of filters. Even people from the same family will have different belief systems.

When we are looking at a cultural belief system we are looking at a dominant set of beliefs of that culture. These dominant sets will vary from culture to culture. Some cultures are similar and some seem poles apart.

There are some basic elements to integrating cultures. Co-operation and contribution are the foundation on which all else sits. Co-operation allows for the different belief systems of others. Respect (which is a part of co-operation) is not imposing your own beliefs on others and the individual rights of others. We all have the same genetic needs and co-operation and contribution to society meet those needs. Respecting the laws and rules of the culture you are in is the foundation for integration.

I wrote earlier about how human beings survived through learning to adapt. When you enter a country with a different culture to the one in which you were born, learning to adapt to this culture makes for happiness. You must adapt to integrate. Adaptation enables integration. Integration facilitates acceptance. Many Greeks and Italians have migrated to Australia, bringing with them a culture rich in food and wine. The British probably introduced fish and chips and beer, the staple diet of my teenage years. This has enhanced the Australian culture by adding to it. We now have a culture rich with all the foods of the world. The contribution and co-operation of new migrants helped build Australia into the country that it is today. New immigrants adapted to new laws and rules and yet at the same time they could enhance the culture of this country by adding to it. Elements of their culture enhance the new culture.

Another thing I like about the culture of Australia is the culture of volunteering time for worthy causes, for the greater community. Every junior sporting club is filled with such volunteers. This is probably the reason why Australians fare so well in sport despite our small population. This is where we see co-operation and contribution coming together to create a culture that benefits all.

> *If the culture of an organisation is one of fear, this will spread like a cancer through the organisation and result in poor morale*

In business the culture of one organisation can be vastly different to another. Often the culture of an organisation is determined by the management and this is the same in a sporting club. In some organisations people are treated like people. In other organisations people are treated like dispensable numbers. This is often transferred into the way they treat their customers, resulting in poor customer service. Profit numbers are often becoming more important than providing a service to the community or developing a positive culture in a company. If the culture of an organisation is one of fear, this will spread like a cancer through the organisation and result in poor morale. If the culture is based on co-operation and contribution this culture will flourish and so will the company. In a company with a culture based on co-operation and contribution, profit will follow like the cart follows the horse. The culture of a company is also reflected in the morale of the people working for it. One person in a position of management can create poor morale in an organisation through disconnecting habits. The boss manager doesn't promote a culture of co-operation and contribution. They created a culture of disconnection and disempowerment and poor morale follows.

We often see managers, who believe they are at the top of the tree but who are only making decisions for the benefit of themselves. Good management realises it begins at the bottom of the tree - the roots that feed the tree to help it flourish. They are the foundation on which the tree grows. There are times when dead branches need to be pruned for the tree to remain healthy. When the roots feed the tree, co-operation and contribution is nature at work. The roots need the branches and leaves and the branches and leaves need the roots. Both are interdependent for the tree to survive and grow. There is no separation and none more important than the other - just as every cell in the body is required to serve its purpose. What purpose? Contribution and co-operation - integrating as part of the whole and not believing it is separate from the whole.

If we begin to look at the culture of a team, we will usually find the same culture in the club. My youngest son plays Australian rules football. Last season, an opponent charged him with an elbow to the face after he had already kicked the ball. He was knocked unconscious and ended up in hospital with a broken jaw in three places. He missed eight games after an operation to fit three plates to his jaw. His opponent received an eight game suspension at the tribunal. They appealed and asked for video footage but the suspension was upheld.

My sons first return game was against the same team. It appalled me to see his jaw being targeted by the opposing players. What appalled me more was the supporters of the other team urging their players to smash him and take him out. My son was quite nonplussed about the situation. He said he had expected it and it was designed to intimidate him. It didn't work and my sons team won on the day. He ended up in hospital again that night and X-ray's showed the plates had moved but another operation was not required. He played the following week.

What surprised me was the aggressive nature of both the players and supporters. What I was seeing was the culture of this club. An aggressive win at all cost culture. To want to see an opponent injured is not the type of culture that will develop a positive mindset in players. It will only encourage unharnessed aggression. The culture of a sporting club starts at management level and filters down through athletes and supporters.

Sportsmanship is **defined** as ethical, appropriate, polite and fair behaviour while participating in a game or athletic event. Any club not cultivating sportsmanship in their athletes can only be coming from a place of fear.

We can also begin to see how the virtues of the samurai bushido code, virtues of rectitude, honor, courage, self-control, politeness and respect come into play here.

There is so much money in sport these days that many athletes look to cheating to give themselves an edge. Cyclist Lance Armstrong comes to mind here. Once considered the greatest cyclist ever is now considered a cheat and stripped of his achievements. There seems to be an ever increasing use of performance enhancing drugs to create an unfair advantage. This is a culture that seems to be building in many sports. I can't see how anyone can gain satisfaction from a win knowing they have cheated. Once you sacrifice your integrity it can be hard to get it back. To lose yourself for a win can only be a detriment to your self-esteem. This is not the mindset of a warrior, it is a mindset based in fear.

Everyone can do their bit to improve the culture of a country, a business, a sporting club or even a family through co-operation and contribution. The virtues of rectitude, honour, courage, self-control, politeness and respect should never be sacrificed. It needs to start with each of us to influence the rest.

The Bushido code was developed as a foundation for Japanese culture. The culture of the nation was based on this moral code of conduct. It was not only the samurai that was expected to follow this code but everyone. Western culture tries to force people into a moral and ethical code of conduct through the laws we make. Older eastern cultures built a code to develop character. A persons character was judged by how they adhered to this moral code of conduct. It was considered a disgrace to break this code of service. Western culture is more about self and ego. Eastern culture was more about community and greater good.

MINDSET OF THE WARRIOR

CHAPTER 30

Strategy, Tactics and the 'Art of War'

From the book *Secret Tactics: Lessons from the Great Masters of Martial Arts.* by Kazumi Tabata.

From book one: The book of Seven Masters is a study of works written between the fifteenth and sixteenth centuries by men who lived by the sword in harsh times and contain valuable lessons for us today.

In studying martial arts the most important factor is not merely to understand but to transcend technique and rationale.

Technique and strategy.

To train technique and strategy until it is a subconscious habit without conscious thought, just confidence and trust. It says the spiritual aspect is most important. That is the psychological grounding that creates a presence of mind.

The ultimate purpose of practicing is to make the art thoroughly a part of oneself. It is necessary to achieve a state where you can use optimum techniques reflexively and unconsciously.

The technique of adapting to circumstances is not achieved using the conscious mind. It is necessary to adjust intuitively according to natural laws, without having to calculate ones movements. One should respect this power within oneself. Practice will make what is conscious, unconscious. Then one will be able to adjust to all situations unconsciously.

True strategy cannot be explained in words, and it cannot be taught through instruction on how to stand and where to strike etc. You must realise it yourself, apart from the instruction you receive from your teacher, then you will be able to act with complete freedom as if there were no rules at all. No one can read the mind of one so free. To learn this truth you must not stay on the level of simple or coarse teachings, but strive towards a higher and more beautiful spirit.

A fight lies in the change of technique. Apply techniques that are beyond the opponents anticipation. Become one with your opponent like a reflection in a mirror. The more one aims to win the more one is likely to fail. When one has no notion of winning one cannot lose. When mind and skill become one, determining victory or defeat becomes irrelevant.

Or in other words, train technique until you don't need to think about it.

It's like a piano player who trains for years in technique. In concert he must abandon all thoughts of technique to let emotion colour the music. He moves from thinking about it to feeling it.

This is focus and intent. Do not allow your soul to be attached to technique.

To avoid being struck is more difficult than to strike. By maintaining a safe distance, an opponents failed attack can be turned to your advantage and allow you to turn your defence into attack.

Once you deliver a first blow don't allow your opponent time to recover. Continue to strike repeatedly. Don't allow your mind to dwell on the first blow. Never imagine you are safe after you deal a blow to an opponent. If your mind dwells on the first blow it becomes inattentive to the opponents counter attack.

A master of strategy is someone who has mastered all techniques and then has given them up altogether. He always acts with his natural state of mind.

If you place your mind on your opponents strike it will be caught by the strike. If you concentrate on timing and distance, you will be caught by timing and distance, your actions will be futile. It is not good to pay attention to your opponents mind or to place your attention on your own body. Whenever the mind is captivated it has stopped, it no longer flows from one moment to the next. The mind must be free to move forward, backward, right and left or in any direction. If your mind becomes fixed on something, judgments of various sorts appear and thoughts race about busily within the mind. This is a mind of attachment.

Grasp the opponents real intention.

Everyone has favourite moves and it is important to recognise an opponent's favourite moves. You can get an opponent off guard by allowing them to throw their favourite moves and counter attack.

For skill to come alive the mind and body must work as one.

A stronger swordsman might take the offensive with a powerful strike to the opponents head to kill. The defender deflects this strike and intuitively with a subtle lunge, cuts the tendon behind his opponents knee or heel. Not returning force with force, but force with guile. A technique he would have trained many times until it became no thought.

He doesn't kill his opponent but renders him defenceless. A strategy to set up the fatal blow.

Rhythm.

An undetermined mind will be dragged into an opponent's rhythm.

Rhythm is especially important, and no one can excel without developing rhythm. Rhythm and tempo must be kept in balance. After discovering your opponent's rhythm you must meet him with an unexpected rhythm. One can win with such strategy.

If an opponent finds the rhythm of your strokes agreeable, he will feel it easier to deliver his strokes. If he has a slow rhythm counter with a fast rhythm. Deliver the kind of strokes that do not harmonise with the opponents strokes. Don't let your opponent find any rhythm, it will unbalance their flow. One you understand the flow of an opponent's motion you can defeat him with greater ease.

Those who understand force can control others, those who don't understand force are controlled by others. To defeat an opponent one must understand and take control of the opponents rhythm.

Everything has its own rhythm. A rise and fall. To avoid fall one needs to get an understanding of the rhythm of fall. Don't compete with the same rhythm as your opponent. Victory comes from a rhythm opposite to that of an opponent.

Mastering the right timing that deflates the rhythm of an opponent and this requires training. Tennis players calling time out might be an example.

STRATEGY, TACTICS AND THE 'ART OF WAR'

Offensive mind in defence : defensive mind in attack.

Offensive opponent

The most important thing is to attack as you defend and to defend as you attack. Whatever circumstance prepare to respond promptly.

Prepare yourself for the offensive opponent by strengthening your mind for defence. Unprepared for his surprise attack you may not have time to bring your full training into play. You must design various strategies to take advantage of an opponent's initial move.

When the outward appearance is spirited, the inner self is calm. When the outward appearance is aggressive, the inner self is defensive. Thus make the state of your inner self the opposite to your outward appearance. Through continuous practice the outer and the inner selves will become one.

Remain calm outside yet alert and prepared inside, keeping a careful balance between outside and inside: A state of mind that will allow you to switch from stillness to action.

When moving into offensive the inter mind should be still and not going along with the exterior. By keeping you mind still you can better control your action. If both inner and outer are active, neither will be under control. Alternate the offence and defence, stillness and action.

Never forget to make your mind work when the body is quiet, and to make your mind calm when your body is in action.

The way I read this is when you are attacking you don't lose sight of the possible need to defend(cautious defensive inner self). When defending, your inner self is looking for opportunities to attack. When both body and mind are on the offensive one often becomes reckless. Through adopting this in practice it becomes subconscious. You therefore protect yourself in attack and turn defence into attack. This is training a tactical mindset that can be employed in any strategy.

Dis-ease.

It is a disease to be possessed by ideas of victory and technique. To be determined to act first or to wait for your opponents move. The disease is a rigid mind and fixed regardless of situation. It is a disease even to try to get rid of the disease. Fixing ones thoughts on expelling a disease is just another disease. Even being possessed by the thought your mind is unsound is such a fixed thought, and therefore a disease.

When one thought removes another, the disease of the mind both the thoughts of removing and the removed thought will vanish forever. A fixed wedge will loosen when another is driven in beside it. The second wedge will also loosen and nothing will remain. The higher level of training is to remove disease by giving up any efforts to remove it. You can't remove a disease by being possessed by the idea of expelling the disease. Trying to remove the disease means keeping it in your mind. Train your mind so as not to be bothered by a disease. A disease is a fixed mind. Disease in this case is dis-ease.

The mind of no thought is called munen. You can reach munen by removing thoughts through the means of other thoughts.

The 2 wedges can be the acceptance of the thoughts "I can't strike, I can strike" until the thoughts of striking fall away. When thoughts of technique drop from your mind it is the position of no thought. Try embracing the opposites to dissolve the thoughts.

No mind.

Ki is said to be a state of mind ready for anything. If Ki is rigid it will restrain the mind and deprive it of freedom. Free action is only possible when the mind is completely free. The mind changes as the environment changes. In martial arts your mental attitude changes as your opponents movements change. You cannot perceive the change because the mind stays nowhere and leaves nothing behind, it cannot be perceived for certain. What is implied is the resting mind will give way to the conventional techniques. The mind that stops changing and becomes rigid will create problems. The human mind becomes visible when it is stained with an emotion or a thought. If you have something on your mind your face reveals it. You will be defeated if you stick to fixed techniques. It is important to train yourself so that you can keep your mind from stopping at one place.

It is important not to stop the mind on anything. Speed results from not stopping the mind. If you stop your mind it will be captured by your opponent. If you move with the intent to be quick your mind will be caught by its own intention.

If you try to control your mind you will be captivated by the thoughts of controlling it. The movement of your mind will be restricted. You should not put your mind anywhere, then it will expand to fill the entire body. The mind will then serve the part of the body that is needed and perform actions as they become necessary. Throw away your mind, your thoughts and judgements, set it free to be. If it is not put in one place it is everywhere. It penetrates the entire body and is extended in all directions. If it is not fixated on one direction it can function in all directions. If the mind does not stop it remains empty, no mind, no thought. In this state the mind will respond to everything and stop on nothing.

For technique to be good, the mind has to be completely abandoned.

It is impossible to calculate the future. So lay aside your thoughts and calculations and look with an empty mind.

Abandoning the attached mind and seeking a state of mindlessness is putting one's mind on a flowing unwavering course.

Ultimate mindfulness is freely allowing the opponent to exercise technique and then rendering them ineffective. Freely move along with the offensive movements of an opponent like flowing water. The mind should be clear yet determined when exercising technique.

Achieving a state devoid of doubt is the essence of martial arts.

The mind free from the want to win or fear of losing allows one to adapt to any situation.

Only the tranquil mind can become capable of free execution of techniques.

In the mind void will appear and actual ability will appear. Both will always appear and disappear. The void is the gap in your opponents defences that gives the opportunity to mount an offensive.

Virtues.

Dignity is being able to overpower an opponent without making a move. Forcefulness is being able to overpower an opponent through ones manoeuvres. Flexibility is being able to adjust ones actions according to the situation. Dignity may appear peaceful but within it is concealed the ability to change and fit any situation. Forcefulness can alter itself when in motion. Face the opponent with dignity and win through strength. Dignity is found in strength and strength is found in dignity.

Just as the notes in music will move through a scale only to return to the same note. The beginner has no knowledge and displays no outward display of wisdom. Similarly, people who have attained higher levels of wisdom do not show their wisdom outwardly. It is often those with superficial knowledge of things who cultivate the appearance of knowledge.

When approaching battle discipline yourself to be dignified at all times. Sharpen your mind and show your dignity.

Your body and mind will not work together if you lack discipline.

The teacher can only teach, it is the student that must gain understanding of the truth himself.

Never have a wicked heart. Train not by thought but by practice, Learn a wide variety of skills and do not fix on one only, Know not only you own techniques but also those of many others. Find out rationally what is an advantage and what is a disadvantage. Foster an intuitive ability to judge all things. Feel and essence that you cannot see on the surface. Pay attention to the smallest of phenomena. Do nothing in vain for the energy and time we have is limited.

To have dignity we must master virtue. The bushido code is a code of virtues. Moral belief is the foundation of dignity. (Expand on this with bushido code and 'art of war').

The three basic situations.

Taking the offensive. There are several ways of attacking. Quick with agility while remaining calm. Strong and fast on the surface with internal calm. Simply empty your mind and concentrate on defeating your opponent.

The smash: When your enemy is weak, inexperienced or his rhythm is off you should pursue him without hesitation and smash him, never allow him to get back to his feet.

Defence. Remain calm and make yourself appear weak, then jump aside and interrupt the rhythm of his attack then counter attack. Show your strength from the beginning and spot the weak points in the attack and take advantage of them.

Both offensive. When you opponent attacks in haste make your own attack quiet and quick. When the opponent attack quietly, be fast and attack with strength.

The rule under most situations you should attack first, if this is not possible wait for the enemy to attack and then take control of the situation.

To be honest with yourself is to recognise there are two conflicting forces in your heart. As much as you want to conquer your opponent you are frightened and want to avoid him. You must learn to quiet your fear and allow the desire to conquer to flow freely from you.

Victory comes from a relaxed state of mind.

Remove all fear and delusion

Mind. Have an undisguised mind and immovable mind

Intention. Have selfless, unmixed and clear intention.

Wind. Have a clear mind and body like a wind when launching an attack.

Water. Flexibly react to the opponents movements like water touching things.

The greatest weapon of all is the human mind, all other things are tools and extensions of it.

'The Art of War' Quotes By Sun Tzu.

The Art of War is an ancient (around 2,500 year old) Chinese military treatise attributed to Sun Tzu, a high ranking military general, strategist and tactician. The following quotes are as true today as they were then proving true knowledge will endure the test of time.

We will cover some of the quotes and suggest you read the translation, *The Art of War* by Thomas Cleary to fully understand this past master.

Deception is the *'art of war'* says Sun Tzu. Deception in this context is the pretense of one strategy, to hide your true strategy. It is an intellectual tactic, which might be seen more as a diversion of interest of the opponent from your true purpose. Like a chess player pretending one strategy with the hidden agenda of luring you into a checkmate position with another strategy.

To lie or distort to deceive for singular personal gain lacks honesty and integrity. It is not virtuous. It has no honour. Deception in the art of war is less a character flaw than an intellectual tactical ploy that is used in

STRATEGY, TACTICS AND THE 'ART OF WAR'

many sports and games.

"Strategy without tactics is the slowest route to victory. Tactics without strategy is the noise before defeat."

"Those skilled at making the enemy move do so by creating a situation to which he must conform; they entice him with something he is certain to take, and with lures of ostensible profit they await him in strength."

"If you know the enemy and know yourself, you need not fear the result of a hundred battles. If you know yourself but not the enemy, for every victory gained you will also suffer a defeat. If you know neither the enemy nor yourself, you will succumb in every battle"

"All warfare is based on deception."

"Appear weak when you are strong, and strong when you are weak."

A strategy is a general, undetailed plan of action, encompassing a period of time, to achieve a complicated goal. A tactic is a conceptual action implemented as one or more specific tasks.

The strategy we employ will probably remain the same from fight to fight. Striking, wrestling, grappling to submission. The tactics will vary depending on opponents skill set and psychology. We can employ deception quite easily. Your opponents will become overconfident because of the three losses, we can exploit this. They will underestimate your stand up abilities. This sets us up to use our strategy. They will become overconfident in striking and wrestling. Remember the shock that Silver got. Your mind set at the time couldn't capitalise on it. You didn't know yourself but now you are starting to understand and know yourself. Your intelligence is superior to your opponents, you will know your enemy more than they will know you. Your strategy and tactics will not be based on overconfidence but logic. Play to your opponents ego to create a weakness. This is the art of war.

"When the enemy is relaxed, make them toil. When full, starve them. When settled, make them move."

"To know your Enemy, you must become your Enemy."

To know the way you enemy thinks is to know they have and ego based in fear. Understand their fears and exploit it. They fear your strengths and underestimate your other abilities. The ego is the easiest thing to exploit.

"Move swift as the Wind and closely-formed as the Wood. Attack like the Fire and be still as the Mountain."

If you become too calm you can lose your intensity, be still in mind and harness intensity. To be as still as a mountain is to be unperturbed by trivialities yet focused. To move as swift as the wind is to change swiftly through intuition and changing situation. To attack like fire is to unleash the power and intensity within when the time is right.

"Engage people with what they expect; it is what they are able to discern and confirms their projections. It settles them into predictable patterns of response, occupying their minds while you wait for the extraordinary moment — that which they cannot anticipate."

Begin the fight the way you have done when you have won fights or lost fights against them or others. Let them think you are predictable before unleashing the unpredictable.

"What the ancients called a clever fighter is one who not only wins, but excels in winning with ease."

Expect to win a fight in the first round easily. If it is round two or three, so be it. You are not there for someone else's entertainment. You are there to show your dominance, demand respect and achieve you're goal.

STRATEGY, TACTICS AND THE 'ART OF WAR'

"There are not more than five musical notes, yet the combinations of these five give rise to more melodies than can ever be heard.

There are not more than five primary colours, yet in combination they produce more hues than can ever been seen.

There are not more than five cardinal tastes, yet combinations of them yield more flavours than can ever be tasted."

Your combination of skills created the melody, colours and flavours of the fight. All dimensions not one dimension.

"If quick, I survive. If not quick, I am lost. This is "death."

Your subconscious is quick, it sees all that is. Trust it.

"He who is prudent and lies in wait for an enemy who is not prudent, will be victorious."

Tactics to strategy. Patience in a game that lacks it.

"Thus the expert in battle moves the enemy, and is not moved by him."

Your tactics move an opponent to a point where strategy is implemented.

"So in war, the way is to avoid what is strong, and strike at what is weak."

Tactics.

"One mark of a great soldier is that he fights on his own terms or fights not at all."

When your tactics lead to your implementation of strategy. You dictate terms.

"In the midst of chaos, there is also opportunity"

Only the still mind of focus and intent can see opportunity in chaos.

"Hence that general is skilful in attack whose opponent does not know what to defend; and he is skilful in defence whose opponent does not know what to attack."

Your stand up game will create confusion in what to defend and what to attack.

"Do not repeat the tactics which have gained you one victory, but let your methods be regulated by the infinite variety of circumstances."

Let you strategy be your base and your tactics be flexible and variable.

"The skilful tactician may be likened to the shuai-jan. Now the shuai-jan is a snake that is found in the Ch'ang mountain's. Strike at its head, and you will be attacked by its tail; strike at its tail, and you will be attacked by its head; strike at its middle, and you will be attacked by head and tail both."

Let your tactics be variable and flexible, Let tactics flow around your strategy.

"Rouse him, and learn the principle of his activity or inactivity. Force him to reveal himself, so as to find out his vulnerable spots."

Feel your opponent out for vulnerability, see no strength but look for vulnerability. Find it and exploit it. Be patient because it will reveal itself in time.

"A clever general, therefore, avoids an army when its spirit is keen, but attacks it when it is sluggish and inclined to return. This is the art of studying moods."

Before a fight the ego wants to fight. When the other ego steps out of the ring it has nothing to fight, it become dispirited. It becomes

sluggish. It has lost its purpose: The mood changes. One of the reasons I mentioned prefight posturing. Don't feed your opponents spirit and determination.

Don't buy into an opponent's aggression and overconfidence. They will pump themselves up through the ego. Don't buy into a battle of the ego's. The inflated ego can deflate like a balloon when pricked with something as small as a pin. It is filled with nothing of substance.

"You can be sure of succeeding in your attacks if you only attack places which are undefended .You can ensure the safety of your defence if you only hold positions that cannot be attacked."

Have patience for an undefended opportunity to attack. Create a defensive position that can only create a position of counter attack.

"Security against defeat implies defensive tactics; ability to defeat the enemy means taking the offensive."

"The consummate leader cultivates the Moral Law, and strictly adheres to method and discipline; thus it is in his power to control success."

Your discipline and method is your strategy, moral virtues your mindset. We are seeing the bushido code of moral virtues employed centuries before the samurai adopted them as a moral code of conduct.

CHAPTER 31

Body Language and Presence

In this chapter on body language we will focus on the fighter with the comments. It can be applied to all competitive sports. We can influence our state of mind by the body language we use. We can use the old saying that a team has *dropped their heads* to understand it's influence. The body language is submissive - they have given up. A change in posture can create a change in mindset. Our body language is unconscious and usually reflects the way we feel or our intention. The body language of one person in a team, can pull down, or lift up others in the team. Our body language is unconscious signals to another person's subconscious. We react to this at a subconscious level even if we don't fully understand why. It is said that 55% of our communication with others is non-verbal - comes through our body language.

It is important for an athletic competitor to communicate his or her confidence and trust through their body language. A competitor can tune into a defensive or submissive body language of an opponent to gain confidence, and often do.

When I see a team briskly running off the field at half time while their opponents sluggishly walk off, it is telling me a great deal about the mindset of both teams.

When a coach berates a player using disconnecting habits it will often result in aggressive or defensive body language in the player. Neither is a good result and can infect the rest of the team.

A coach's body language is also important in what it communicates to the team. To see a coach with his head in his hands while shaking his head, will not instil confidence and trust in his athletes. If you tell an athlete they can't, they cant. If you tell them they can, they can. Surprisingly, it is often communicated without saying a word. I think it is important for athlete's to learn to develop a presence of confidence and trust, and show it in their body language. This is what you want to communicate to an opponent's subconscious.

Presence.

Presence is the combination of confidence and trust. Our body language reflects our confidence and trust through the presence we exude through a lack of wants and a positive expectation. It is non-aggressive.

Understanding body language has a number of advantages. It lets us perceive our opponents subconscious mindset and motives. We can use this and choose our own body language as a tactic to create a perception in their mindset. Deception is the art of war. The below information is general to get a general understanding. I add comments as possible tactics for the fighter.

Many fighters are multi-dimensional in skills but one dimensional in attitude. Aggressive posturing to intimidate. Both in and out of the ring against opponents. The goal is to see this as a weakness and exploit it. By exerting body language that is dominant but not aggressive.

Body language is subconscious. The person doesn't know they are doing it. When you study an opponent you should study their pre-fight body language and body language during a fight. In a fight, look for their attack signals. You should see a change in facial expression, fists clenching, change in posture etc. Look for habitual behaviour before the doing of something. An example might be a boxer tapping his glove on his temple just before striking. Their unconscious habits telegraph their behaviour. It makes them predictable.

The following definitions of body language come from the web site www.changingminds.org and with kind permission from David Straker

Aggressive Body Language

A significant cluster of body movements is used to signal aggression. This can come from a fear of attack and be defensive in its nature: it is the want to control another.

<u>Aggressive pre-fight posturing</u>

This can come from a grudge, desire to intimidate, or showmanship to fire up the crowd. With the exception of showmanship, it comes from the ego. The ego with aggression and intimidation can take a fighter or an athlete a long way and lift one up to high levels. The reverse side of the coin is that it can drag them down if they lose. You can use any aggression you feel from a loss to train and work harder and use it to your advantage by creating a more determined mind set, as many will, but this might only give a distorted sense of confidence if the ego isn't over the loss. The confidence will lack trust. If you feel the showmanship of posturing is a better fit for you psychologically, tactically and financially, then use it. But don't let the ego be attached to it.

Masculine energy shows itself as an unstated power, strength, presence of mind and assertiveness. Aggression comes mostly from a point of fear and lack of discipline if it isn't harnessed. It's the want to control.

Threat

Facial signals

Much aggression can be shown in the face, from disapproving frowns and pursed lips to sneers and full snarls. The eyes can be used to stare and hold the gaze for long period. They may also squint, preventing the other person seeing where you are looking.

We can use an emotionless stare to create a sense of power that is not intimidated. It creates an uncertainty in your opponent at a subconscious level.

Attack signals

When somebody is about to attack, they give visual signal such as clenching of fists ready to strike and lowering and spreading of the body for stability. They are also likely to give anger signs such as redness of the face.

Learning to read this body language can become automatic. It telegraphs their intent. You see their thoughts at a subconscious level before they act.

Exposing oneself

Exposing oneself to attack is also a form of aggression. It is saying 'Go on - I dare you. I will still win.' It can include not looking at the other person, dropping arms, dropping defence , relaxing the body, turning away and so on.

This can also come from a point of power. It can be a tactic used instigate attack by them and then counterattack by you if used the right way. Best used when you have the upper hand in a fight to show confidence.

Invasion

Invading the space of the other person in some way is an act of aggression that is equivalent to one country invading another. An intimate comfort zone will be 6" to 18" reserved for partners, children and some family. The friend comfort zone goes from 18" to 4 foot. (150mm to 450mm and 450mm to 1.2m.)

Aggressive posturing comes from this. It will often fire up the other person's ego in defence and create a battle of the ego's if you buy into it. If they enter your space stand firm without emotion but with confidence and trust. Most people will become aggressive or submissive if you enter their space.

False friendship

Invasion is often done under the cloak of familiarity, where you act as if you are being friendly and move into a space reserved for friends, but *without being invited*. This gives the other person a dilemma of whether to repel a 'friendly' advance or to accept dominance of the other.

In most cases this will be rejected in a situation of competition. People often invade another's space with aggressive body language while apologising. Mouth saying sorry and body and eyes saying I don't really care.

Approach

When you go inside the comfort zone of others without permission, you are effectively invading their territory. The closer you get, the greater your ability to have 'first strike', from which an opponent may not recover. This creates the discomfort they feel.

If you are entering their comfort zone they will feel discomfort you are invading first strike. If they are entering yours you can feel discomfort

because they are invading, unless you welcome them in because that is your tactic.

Gestures

Insulting gestures

There are many, many <u>gestures</u> that have the primary intent of insulting the other person and hence inciting them to anger and a perhaps unwise battle. Single and double fingers pointed up, a smirk, a snarl, arm thrusts, chin tilts, invading a person's comfort zone. Staring for long periods and so on are used.

This is aggressive posturing.

Mock attacks

Gestures may include symbolic action that mimics actual attacks, including waving fingers (the beating baton), shaking fists, head-butts, leg-swinging and so on. This is saying 'Here is what I will do to you!'

Physical items may be used as substitutes, for example banging of tables and doors or throwing things. Again, this is saying 'This could be you!'

This is ego posturing unless mock attacks are designed to create opportunity by eliciting a response, reaction or change in direction. Pretending to do one thing then doing another. Mock attack has no intent other than to intimidate, calculated pretence is a tactical intent to create opportunity.

Sudden movements

All of these gestures may be done suddenly, signalling your level of aggression and testing the other person's reactions.

Sudden movements from unharnessed aggression might have purpose and intent and be a tactic, but have no have no strategy, other than force and overwhelm. Sudden movements from purpose, intent,

tactics and strategy are designed to create opportunities. Unleashed aggression.

Assertive Body Language

<u>Assertiveness</u> is about acting in an 'adult' manner, asserting your rights without <u>aggression</u> and without being <u>submissive</u>.

Smooth

Assertive body language is not jerky and tense. Nor is it held still under close control. It moves at a steady rate, indicating that the person is feeling relatively relaxed. Even when they are speaking passionately, the movement is still smooth and under control.

A smooth voice is natural and even. It goes up and down in time with the words, matching the expression. The sound is warm, friendly and melodious. Vocal volume goes up and down evenly, not suddenly becoming loud or quiet.

When the person looks around they do so in steady sweeps. They do not have eyes that dart about furtively nor do they stare nor are they downcast.

Assertiveness comes from a point of personal power, from a point of confidence and trust. Being aggressive or submissive comes from a point of fear.

Balanced

A balanced body is upright and relaxed. Bones rest on one another, held in place by gravity, rather than leaning outward and hence having to be held together with muscular strength. Both sides of the body are used, hence both hands may be used together or in balanced sequence. A balanced voice does not go to extremes. It is not jagged nor is it monotonous. It goes up and down in a natural way that sounds honest and persuasive.

Aggressiveness drains energy, assertiveness conserves energy to be released when the time is right. It flows up and down in a natural way.

Firm

When we assert something we act as if is true. Feet are firmly planted, flat on the floor (including when sitting), typically slightly apart to provide a firm base.

Gestures are used to <u>emphasize</u> truths, although not in an exaggerated way. Hence the head nods, outstretched forearms bounce downwards with the point and the body may lean slightly forwards.

There is also firmness in response where the other person may attempt to dominate or avoid the point. Gentle touching may be used as encouragement and steady eye contact used to show determination. Rejection of things not wanted is done steadily and without the escalation of aggression nor with the weakness of a passive position.

Aggression is avoided, particularly in facial expressions, which are gentle and concerned yet show a determination to see things through.

Unharnessed aggression closes down our perception of reality from a base of fear. We are firm in our resolve when we assert something and act as if is true.

Open

The body language is <u>open</u>, showing no threat and fearlessly inviting response. There are no barriers across the body. Arms hang down or are held outwards. Hands are often palms-up rather than fists or placating palms down.

Eye contact is regular and appropriate. There is neither aggressive staring at the other person nor are eyes submissively downcast. There is no hiding of the face or body and barriers are removed.

Openness includes smiling, accepting and <u>listening</u>. The assertive person is attentive and checks that they have understood what the other person has said. They also respond to the concerns of others, showing this in their body language.

Use open body language to show no fear of threat and fearlessly inviting response. Be open pre-fight. Look for your opponent closed language.

Closed Body Language

A significant cluster of body movements are all about *closing*. This is sometimes misinterpreted solely as indicating defensiveness.

Language of closure

Closure literally closes the body up. It may range from a slight bringing together of the limbs to curled up into a tight ball. Extreme cases may also include rhythmic rocking of the body to and fro.

Arms across

In a closed positions one or both arms cross the central line of the body. They may be folded or tightly clasped or holding one another. There may also be holding one another.

Lighter arm crossing may include resting an arm on a table or leg, or loosely crossed with wrists crossing.

Varying levels of tension may be seen in the arms and shoulders, from a relaxed droop to tight tension and holding on to the body or other arms.

Legs across

Legs, likewise can be crossed. There are several styles of leg crossing, including the ankle cross, the knee cross, the figure-four (ankle on opposite knee) and the tense wrap-around.

Legs may also wrap around convenient other objects, such as chair legs.

When legs are crossed but arms are not, it can show deliberate attempts to appear relaxed. This is particularly true when legs are hidden under a table.

Looking down or away

The head may be inclined away from the person, and particularly may be tucked down.

Closure indicates tension, nervousness and defence. The more open you are and the more closed your opponent is pre-fight the more nervous they will become.

Defensive Body Language

When a person is feeling threatened in some ways, they will take defensive body postures.

Defending from attack

The basic defensive body language has a primitive basis and assumes that the other person will physically attack, even when this is highly unlikely.

Covering vital organs and points of vulnerability

In physical defence, the defensive person will automatically tend to cover those parts of the body that could be damaged by an attack.

The chin is held down, covering the neck. The groin is protected with knees together, crossed legs or covering with hands. The arms may be held across the chest or face.

Fending off

Arms may be held out to fend off attacker, possibly straight out or curved to deflect incoming attacks.

Using a barrier

Any physical object may be placed held in front of the person to act as a literal or figurative barrier. This can be a small as a pen or as large as a table. Straddling a reversed chair makes some people comfortable in conversation as they look relaxed whilst feeling defensive.

The barrier may be static, such as a desk or may be carried, from a pen held in front (maybe with both hands) to a hugged cushion or crossed arms. This is one reason why children may carry toys around, held close in front of them.

Barriers can also protect the other person and if I am powerful, I may use a simple barrier to make you feel less defensive. It also means I control the barrier.

Becoming small

One way of defending against attack is to reduce the size of the target. People may thus huddle into a smaller position, keeping their arms and legs in.

Rigidity

Another primitive response is to tense up, making the muscles harder in order to withstand a physical attack.

Rigidity also freezes the body, possibly avoiding movements being noticed or being interpreted as preparing for attack.

Hiding

People who are feeling vulnerable will tend to move to safe places, for example walking on the inside of the sidewalk, away from the road, or just staying indoors in familiar environments.

When they are in vulnerable positions, they may be seen to be using more protective body language, hunching down, wrapping arms together and so on.

Seeking escape

Flicking the eyes from side to side shows that the person is looking for a way out.

Defensive body language is the mind resigned to defeat. Like the rabbit stuck in the headlights of a car. Recognise this in your opponent and take the opportunity to dominate and finish the fight. Miss the signals and you won't capitalise on them. You can also use this body language to bring your opponent in for an unexpected counter attack. Deception.

Pre-empting attack

Giving in

Pre-empting the attack, the defensive person may reduce their position, generally using submissive body language, avoiding looking at the other person, keeping the head down and possibly crouching into a lower body position.

Attacking first

Aggressive body language may also appear, as the person uses 'attack as the best form of defence'. The body may thus be erect, thrust forward and with attacking movements.

Where attack and defence both appear together, there may be conflicting signs appearing together. Thus the upper body may exhibit aggression whilst the legs are twisted together.

Both these cases come from a defensive mindset and not from a point of tactics or strategy.

Dominant Body Language

Dominant body language is related to <u>aggressive body language</u>, though with a less emotional content.

Size signals

The body in dominant stances is generally <u>open</u>, and may also include additional aspects.

Making the body big

Hands on hips makes the elbows go wide and make the body seem larger. So also does standing upright and erect, with the chin up and the chest thrust out. Legs may be placed apart to increase size.

Making the body high

Height is also important as it gives an attack advantage. This can be achieved by standing up straight or somehow getting the other person lower than you, for example by putting them on a lower seat or by your standing on a step or plinth.

Occupying territory

By invading and occupying territory that others may own or use, control and dominance is indicated. A dominant person may thus stand with feet apart and hands on hips.

Dominant body language is a presence of confidence and trust in yourself. Feel big and feel powerful.

Superiority signals

Breaking social rules

Rulers do not need to follow rules: they *make* the rules. This power to decide one's own path is often displayed in breaking of social rules, from invasion and interruption to casual swearing in polite company.

Ownership

Owning something that others covet provides a status symbol. This can be territorial, such as a larger office, or displays of wealth or power, such as a Rolex watch or having many subordinates.

Just owning things is an initial symbol, but in body language it is the flaunting of these, often casually, that is the power display. Thus a senior manager will casually take out their Mont Blanc pen whilst telling their secretary to fetch the Havana cigars.

Invasion

A dominant act is to disrespect the ownership of others, invading their territory, for example getting too close to them by moving into their body space. Other actions include sitting on their chairs, leaning on their cars, putting feet up on their furniture and being over-friendly with their romantic partners.

Invasion says 'What's yours is mine' and 'I can take anything of yours that I want and you cannot stop me'.

Dominant positions

A dominant person will take higher status physical positions where they can see and be seen by more other people.

If the table is rectangular, they will sit at the end. Likewise, they will sit on a corner seat. They will also stand in the middle of a group where they will have their backs to some people (but will not fear attack).

They will also walk down the middle of a path or corridor and expect others to get out of the way. Negotiations for moving over start a long way off and they signal by not making any moves that others will have to move.

Dominating time

Dominant people will seek to control time more. For example in conversations, they may talk more themselves and deny others time to talk, for example by interruption or leaving early.

Another method is hurrying, talking fast themselves, checking the time and asking that others 'be brief'.

Outside of conversations, they may not be available when you need them but then demand your attention immediately.

Belittling others

Superiority signals are found both in saying 'I am important' and also 'You are not important'. Thus a dominant person may ignore or interrupt another person who is speaking or turn away from them. They may criticize the inferior person, including when the other person can hear them.

They may inspect their fingernails or otherwise show limited attention to the other person. General preening can likewise show a lack of respect. Stroking the chin shows judgement.

Facial signals

Much dominance can be shown in the face, from disapproving frowns and pursed lips to sneers and snarls (sometimes disguised as smiles).

The eyes can be used to stare and hold the gaze for long period. They may also squint, preventing the other person seeing where you are looking. They may also look anywhere but at the other person, effectively saying that 'you are not even worth looking at'. Narrowing eyes shows suspicion or even dislike.

Faces can also look bored, amused or express other expressions that belittle the other person. The head will often move very little.

A surprisingly effective trick is in holding the head still. Most people move their head as they talk and interact with others. We watch the faces of others a great deal and stillness in the head and face signals comfort and lack of anxiety.

Dominant people often smile much less than submissive people.

No one is superior to another other than in the ego. The ego wants to feel superior and so must feel inferior. Knowing this you can exploit your opponents want to feel superior to make them feel inferior if you don't buy into the battle of the ego. A pricked ego can become more aggressive so be careful how you use this information.

The dominant greeting

When people first meet and greet, their first interaction sets the pattern for the future relationship. When a person is dominant here, then they will most likely continue to be dominant.

The handshake

A classic dominant handshake is with the palm down, symbolically being on top. Another form of dominant handshake is to use strength to squeeze the other person. Holding the other person's hand for longer than normal also shows that you are in control.

Eyes

Prolonged, unblinking eye contact acts like overplaying the handshake -- it says 'I am powerful, I can break the rules.' The dominant person may alternatively prevent eye contact, saying 'You are beneath me and I do not want even to look at you.'

Speaking

The person who speaks first often gets to control the conversation, either by talking for longer or by managing the questions.

And...

It has been found that just putting the body in a dominant position, upright and open, reduces a person's sensitivity to pain, possibly because this increases the sense of <u>control</u>.

Carney, Cuddy and Yap (2010) also found that adopting a powerful pose changes your hormonal levels and increases your propensity to take risks, just as if you were more powerful.

A dominant posture changes body chemistry and sensitivity to pain.

Responding to dominance

If others display dominant body language you have a range of options.

The simplest response is simply not to submit, which is what they probably want. Continue to appear friendly and ignore their subtle signals.

Another response is to fight dominance with dominance, for example:

Out-stare them (a trick here is to look at the bridge of their nose, not their eyes).

Touch them, either before they touch you or immediately when they touch you.

When they do a power handshake, grab their elbow and step to the side.

When they butt in to your speech, speed up, talk more loudly and say 'let me finish!'

Another approach is to name the game. Ask them why they are using dominant body language. A good way to do this is in a curious, unafraid way

You do not submit if you stay open an retain your own unemotional non-aggressive dominance.

Power Body Language

Power is often expressed in communication as a combination of strength and humanity. This is very attractive and is a form of Hurt and Rescue.

Greeting

Handshake

As the other person approaches, move to left side, extend your arm horizontally, palm down (be first to do this). Grab their palm firmly, pull them in and hold their elbow with your left hand.

The horizontal arm is an unmissable signal. Palm on top is being dominant, putting yourself on top. Holding the elbow further controls them. The *royal handshake* is outstretched arm to keep the other at their distance. A limp hand, palm down, stops them doing a power shake.

Touching

Touching is power symbol. Touching people can be threatening, and is used by leaders to demonstrate power. The handshake is, of course, a touch, and can lead to further touching, such as the elbow grip and patting shoulders and back. Guide people with a palm in the small of the back. Greet them with a hand on the back. Touch them on the elbow or other 'safe' areas.

Speaking

Talking

Talk with confidence and use the body beat in time with assertions. Beat with a finger, a palm or even a fist (which is rather aggressive). Emphasize and exaggerate your points.

Use silences too. Pause in the middle of speaking and look around at everyone. If you are not interrupted they are probably respecting your power. Stand confidently without speaking. Look around, gazing into people's eyes for slightly longer than usual.

Emoting

It is powerful to show that you have emotion, but in the right place only. It shows you are human. At other times it emphasizes how you are in control. A neat trick is to bite the lower lip, as it shows both emotion and control (Bill Clinton did it 15 times in 2 minutes during the Monica Lewinsky 'confession').

And...

Walking

Walk with exaggerated swinging of arms, palm down and out. Kink elbows outwards, making the body seem wider. Add a slight swagger.

When walking with others, be in front of them. When going through doors, if you are going to an audience, go first. If you are going from an audience, go last (guiding others through shows dominance).

Position

Generally be higher. Sit on a higher chair. Stand over people. Wear heels. Drive a higher car.

Prefight and interview body language.

Submissive Body Language

A significant cluster of body movements is used to signal fear and readiness to submit.

This is common in animals, where fighting (that could terminally harm each animal) is avoided by displays of <u>aggression</u> or submission.

Body positions

The body in fearful stances is generally <u>closed</u>, and may also include additional aspects.

Self-protection

Hunching inwards reduces the size of the body, limiting the potential of being hit and protecting vital areas, for example hands covering crotch, or chin pushed down to protect the neck.

In a natural setting, being small may also reduce the chance of being seen. Arms are held in. A crouching position may be taken, even slightly with knees slightly bent. This is approaching the curled-up regressive foetal position.

Lowering

Putting the body in a lower position shows the other person that you are not a physical threat. This can include hunching down, bowing, kneeling or even prostration. It is no surprise that these are typically used in formal greetings of a superior person.

Even in sitting, a submissive person will choose a lower chair or slump in order to be lower than others.

Motionlessness

By staying still, the chance of being seen is, in a natural setting, reduced (which is why many animals freeze when they are fearful). When exposed, it also reduces the chance of accidentally sending signals which may be interpreted as being aggressive. It also signals submission in that you are ready to be struck and will not fight back.

Head

Head down

Turning the chin and head down protects the vulnerable neck from attack. It also avoids looking the other person in the face (staring is a sign of aggression).

Eyes

Widening the eyes makes you look more like a baby and hence signals your vulnerability. Looking attentively at the other person shows that you are hanging on their every word.

Mouth

Submissive people smile more at dominant people, but they often smile with the mouth but not with the eyes.

Gestures

Submissive gestures

There are many gestures that have the primary intent of showing submission and that there is no intent to harm the other person. Hands out and palms up shows that no weapons are held and is a common pleading gesture.

Other gestures and actions that indicate tension may indicate the state of fear. This includes hair tugging, face touching and jerky movement. There may also be signs such as whiteness of the face and sweating.

Small gestures

When the submissive person must move, then small gestures are often made. These may be slow to avoid alarming the other person, although tension may make them jerky

Like defensive body language, submissive is the mind resigned to defeat. Like the rabbit stuck in the headlights of a car. Recognise this in your opponent and take the opportunity to dominate and finish the fight. Miss the signals and you won't capitalise on them. You can also use this body language to bring your opponent in for an unexpected counter attack. Deception.

CHAPTER 32

Self-talk and Affirmations

Words we use

Some emotional words will trigger the subconscious emotions they describe. Say you are frustrated about something and you will feel frustrated. Say you are angry about something and you will trigger that emotion. Hate is one of the most distorted words we use and one of the strongest emotional triggers. People use it to describe a food they don't like or the weather. You wouldn't hate that piece of food if you were starving.

Your self-talk is suggestions to the subconscious. The disconnecting habits disconnect both the user and the person they are being used on. They are a knife that cuts both ways. Use them on yourself and you reinforce the ego and your fears, the wants for approval, control and security.

Remove negative emotional self-talk from your vocabulary. Talk yourself up, not down. Don't become your own biggest critic, it will only reinforce negative beliefs.

Affirmations

Affirmations are basically a program of positive self-talk. They are also specific to your sport and your goals. Affirmations should be seen as affirming your goal as though it is already true. Affirmations start to work at a level of belief and reinforce positive beliefs. The imagination can't tell the difference between a real or imagined experience and affirmations create a positive imagination. Affirmations are self-suggestions and repeated self-suggestions is self-hypnosis. I hope you also realize by now that negative self-talk is also negative self-hypnosis.

Affirmations should be recorded and listened to repeatedly. (You can do this on your phone).They should be present tense (I am) not future tense (I will be). They should be phrased with an expectation not a want. The words should all be positive and negative emotional words should be avoided. Phrases should be repeated often but dispersed through the recording. Try to say the same thing in three different ways. This is called a trilogy of suggestions and makes the suggestions more effective.

Here is an example of a few affirmations.

I feed my determination and become more determined every day and in every way.

I have a passion for excellence and I feed it daily.

I Feel full of Confidence.

I ooze Confidence in my skillset.

SELF-TALK AND AFFIRMATIONS

I am Confident in my Skills, Techniques and Abilities.

I am Confident in my Speed, Strength and Stamina.

I am Confident in my Intelligence and Mental Game.

I feel Confident in my Striking, Wrestling and Jiu Jitsu.

I Believe in my Skills, Coaches and Team.

I have Pure and Complete Focus.

I Fight with a Purpose and Intent. It is ingrained in me.

I see no obstacles, only possibilities and opportunities.

I ooze a presence of confidence and trust, knowing my purpose and intent is unshakable.

I am magnanimous in Victory.

My purpose and intent make me fearless.

I pursue my destiny with purpose and intent. Nothing can intimidate or deter me from my goals and destiny.

I enjoy the journey as I create MY own destiny through your purpose and intent.

Whatever does not kill me makes me Stronger; and more determined.

Your instructions to your mind are the parameters the subconscious mind will operate within. The construction and reasoning are operating subconsciously. If we entertain doubts and fears over a period of time the instructions also become automatic and habitual. The mind will find all the ways it can to agree with the instructions you are giving it creating a constructed fantasy and reasoning it to be true. If untested by logic and habitual, it will eventually become the way you see you're world. FEAR - False Evidence Appearing Real.

To overcome fear and doubts we need to create habitual positive thinking. Affirmations and continuing positive self-talk is the only way to do this. If doubts and fears arise in the mind, dismiss them, ignore them and forget them. If you don't give them any energy they will begin to disappear. Then use affirmations and positive self-talk to replace them.

CHAPTER 33

Developing Mindset

Developing Mindset

Subconscious v conscious mind

When sparring, practice just being in the moment. Plant any strategy in your subconscious before sparring or between rounds and expect it to deliver. Visualize a variety of possibilities from a starting strategy then hand it to your subconscious with a positive expectation. Develop an anchor and trigger to bring you back in the moment and switch the conscious mind off. Trust your subconscious will deliver. If you want a cup of coffee you plant the goal through the conscious mind, the subconscious does the rest. It takes you to the kitchen, turns on the kettle, gets the cup, coffee, milk and sugar to your liking, all without a conscious thought. Plant the goal in the subconscious and allow it the flexibility to deliver.

Negative emotions - Fears.

Wants for our approval, control, security and escape are irrational Illogical fears to let go of. Become care free about these fears but don't care less about what you want to achieve. Practice the releasing negative emotions technique until it becomes a habit in all situations. There are many situations in life outside fighting that you can use to practice this. This allows you to go with the flow of life and not fight against it. It will lift your vibrational frequency and energy. Negative emotions are from a lower vibrational frequency and drain energy. Letting go comes from allowance and acceptance without attachment then moving to positive expectation.

Confidence, Trust and Presence.

Develop your presence through confidence and trust in your abilities and a lack of wants. Your presence is your mindset. It should be developed not by wanting an outcome but with the positive expectation of an outcome without attachment or doubt. It is masculine energy with harnessed aggression. It is assertiveness. It is a state of being not a state of wanting. In this state you can't be intimidated.

Attitude

Ability is what you're capable of doing. Motivation determines what you do. Attitude determines how well you do it. A positive attitude comes from not dwelling on the past and doing what you need to do in the present to create your future. It comes from optimism due to learning's from the past, a negative attitude is pessimistic. It holds onto past problems and perceived failures. Learn from the past and dismiss, ignore or just forget the negatives. Then let them go. Become more determined through what you learn from the past never to repeat it again. Let your determination fuel a positive unshakable attitude in the now. Right attitude is a habit to develop in all areas. Many people have a pessimistic attitude because they feel they are a victim of life, not realizing they have become a victim of their own ego. Learn, adjust and drop it.

Purpose and Motivation, Goals and imagination

Write your goals down with a clear purpose. Write them down as though they are already achieved.

Live them every day in your imagination. Imagine them and get the feelings you would have as though they are already achieved. This should be foremost in your mind each day. It is the emotion you would feel when reaching the goal that creates the motivation to reach it.

MINDSET OF THE WARRIOR

CHAPTER 34

The Bushido Code for the Modern Warrior

I think by now you will understand that a life without some sort of ethical and moral discipline will not be a happy life. Through an ethical moral life you meet your needs. Without it you will frustrate them. Life is not easy, it takes courage to be strong in what is right and wrong. Being strong in what you want is not being strong in what you need. It is a small point but makes an enormous difference in your perspective of life - To your ego, or to your true self. Be true to yourself. Without it you are nothing of any substance, because the ego is nothing more than irrational fears. Nothing more than scary shadows on a wall to a child.

The eight virtues of bushido are: Rectitude or justice, Courage, Benevolence and Mercy, Politeness and Respect, Honesty and Sincerity, Honour, Loyalty and Character and Self-control: The foundation of the warrior mindset is to be magnanimous.

To be Magnanimous is to be courageously noble in mind and heart. Generous in forgiving; eschewing resentment or revenge; unselfish.

Being noble of mind and heart. Forgiving against a rival or someone less powerful. Forgiveness against injury or insult. To let go is to be magnanimous. The ego is not magnanimous, it's the bad wolf holding on. The good wolf is magnanimous. It lets go. This is character that rises above the ego. The true self. Look forward to tomorrow, the past is gone and no longer exists, tomorrow is a new day and the start of the rest of your life, and life is good. See it, believe it and live it.

A man that has never experienced any problems or failures in life is a man that has never lived and never learned anything.

Life has its ups and downs, its twists and turns. Nothing is permanent. It is a process of evolution. From Chaos comes order. From order it eventually turns to chaos. Evolution. Enjoy the journey and go with the flow of life. We evolve more quickly through points of chaos.

Rectitude or justice

Rectitude can be described as morally correct thinking and behaviour - Integrity; honesty; righteousness; straightforwardness. This is considered the strongest virtue of the bushido code, the virtue on which all others rest.

The corner stone in rational and logical behaviour must have its basics in how we think. Our understand through modern psychology, is that we meet our needs and the needs of others through morally correct behaviour and thinking. To develop a mind free of fear we must cultivate this above all other.

Courage

Courage is doing what is right, and this is the difference between bravery and courage in the bushido code. Courage is a virtue if it is employed through the virtue of rectitude. Knowing what is right and not doing it displays a lack of courage. It takes courage to live with integrity and honesty.

Benevolence and Mercy

Benevolence and mercy are acts of kindness and the desire to do good for others; goodwill towards others and charitableness. It is often said that the highest requirement of a ruler of men is benevolence. Love, affection for others, generosity, pity and sympathy are traits of benevolence. To be forgiving of insults and injury and free from petty resentfulness or vindictiveness, to be magnanimous and noble of mind is the mindset of the samurai.

Benevolence and mercy come from a point of love and compassion. There are only two types of emotion - love based and fear based. To create a mindset free from fear we must cultivate benevolence and mercy.

Politeness and Respect

Respect is esteem and a sense of worth for another person or a person's position. This virtue is based in benevolence with regards to the feelings of others. Being polite and respectful is not to be done just for the sake of good manners but as a benevolent regard for the feelings of others.

Using connecting habits on a person comes from politeness and respect. Disconnecting habit show a lack of politeness and respect.

Honesty and Sincerity

Honesty and sincerity is the freedom from deceit, hypocrisy, or duplicity in intention, action and communication. It is being truthful upright and fair.

Without honesty and sincerity we have no integrity, no honour. You sacrifice your own self-esteem if you have no ethical code of conduct. To lie is just the want to control something or someone – it is based in fear and nothing more.

Honour

Honour is honesty, or integrity in one's beliefs and actions. Honour not only as a warrior, but also in non-martial behavior. A sense of honour is a sense of personal dignity and worth.

How can you achieve greatness without honour. You might achieve some things without honour but there achievement will be hollow. To sacrifice your personal dignity and self-worth is the greatest sacrifice of all. To cheat in sport through drugs or other means will create hollow victories. There is no honour in cheating.

Loyalty

True men and women remain loyal to the people they are indebted to. It is faithfulness to commitments and obligations. In the mind of the samurai, it is through the importance of honour that lies at the core of loyalty.

If there is no honour there can be no loyalty. In sport you can have many perceived loyal friends when you are at the top of your game, those without honour will soon desert you when things are not going so good. Those with honour will still remain true to you. A slump in your performance can often be an opportunity to sort the wheat from the chaff. The true friends and the hangers on.

Character and self-control

The moral and ethical qualities of a person make up their character. Qualities of honesty, courage and integrity form a person's character. The first objective of a samurai's education was to build up character. Bushido teaches a moral standard of rules for the behavior of the samurai to build character and self-control. Compassion over confrontation and benevolence over belligerence were seen as manly, not weak. It was expected the samurai should know the difference between what is right and what is wrong in both thinking and action. Even being impatient and quick to anger was seen as poor self-control and of inferior character. Unharnessed aggression was seen as a weakness. It is this building of character through the moral compass of bushido that creates the warrior mindset of the samurai. It is a mindset without doubt or fear; without indecision; through virtues of rectitude or justice - courage - benevolence and mercy - politeness and respect - honesty and sincerity - honour - loyalty - character and self-control.

It can be proven just as true today through modern psychology as it was for the samurai. To be free of irrational fear, you need a moral and ethical compass guiding your way. The basis of good character and self-control comes from a code moral and ethical behaviour. To develop the mind of no mind, you must integrated a moral and ethical belief system that frees your mind from fear and doubt. The true mindset of the warrior is based on this.

The mind is neuro-plastic - not set in stone. We can train the mind as well as the body to achieve great things, regardless of our thinking in the past. The mind is the tool of creation. Change your mind and you change everything about your life. Spend as much time training your mind as you do your body and you will see the results.

We can see from a modern psychological view the basis of most fears is the want for approval, control, security and escape. Irrational and illogical fears. By creating a mindset based on moral and ethical principles we free our mind from these wants – we are meeting our needs. This will impact in all areas of your life, not just your sport.

The great masters of the past were considered masters or a reason.

Be courageously noble in mind and heart. It takes courage to let go.

What I am presenting here is how the Bushido code of virtues was an effective way of freeing the mind for the task at hand without doubt or fear. To free the mind from ego and allow the body to flow in the moment. I am not suggesting that we are free of ego, we admit and accept out failings, and we will continue to learn from them. Modern psychology supports the cultivation of these virtues. This is a journey of evolution. To become more human and less reactive to our animal instincts and as a result perform at our optimum level, both in sport and in life. Good sportsmanship requires a moral and ethical code of conduct. I wish you success in both.

ABOUT THE AUTHOR

Anthony Gilmour.

Anthony Gilmour is a practicing Psychotherapist who has been in private practice for over 17 years. Tony specializes in depression, anxiety and sport performance, but suggest most problems athletes face is performance anxiety. He has seen clients from a number of sports, Soccer, cricket, baseball, boxing, mixed martial arts, golf, Tennis, athletics, moto cross riding and many more.

Author of the book 'Tragic to Magic' A book on depression and anxiety and the tools needed to turn this around.

We learn our lessons from the past. If we don't learn from them we are doomed to repeat them. We went back to the past to look at performance psychology of warriors - the mindset. It is amazing that teachings of the past fit in with the psychological understandings of today.

The sword of the Samurai is considered the greatest sword ever made. A many folded soft core that will bend and a sharp hardened edge that can chip but the edge remains intact, the chip is confined so that only a small portion of the blade will chip without destroying the blades ability in conflict. Our focus must be sharp. We must learn to be flexible when being flexible is necessary, but our focus must be sharp. The sword is just as effective when chipped.

The Bushido code is the soft core that all else relies on – the foundation. The edge is how we use it.

www.ingramcontent.com/pod-product-compliance
Lightning Source LLC
Chambersburg PA
CBHW051045160426
43193CB00010B/1078